Prairie PHOENIX

Lilium philadelphicum

THE RED LILY IN SASKATCHEWAN

Prairie PHOENIX

Lilium philadelphicum

THE RED LILY IN SASKATCHEWAN

By
Bonnie J. Lawrence and Anna L. Leighton

Nature Saskatchewan
206 - 1860 Lorne St.
Regina, Saskatchewan S4P 2L7

Special Publication No. 25

Published by Nature Saskatchewan, Special Publication No. 25

Lawrence, Bonnie J. (1953 -   )

Prairie Phoenix: The Red Lily, *Lilium philadelphicum*, in Saskatchewan

Includes bibliographical references

ISBN: 0-921104-21-9

1. Western red lily—Saskatchewan. I. Leighton, Anna L.
II. Nature Saskatchewan III. Title.

QK495.L72L39 2005   584'.3   C2005-902087-3

Cover design and book design by Yves Noblet, The Noblet Design Group, Regina, Saskatchewan

Printed and bound in Canada at Friesens Corporation, Altona, Manitoba

Front cover photograph: Red Lily flower by George Tosh

Back cover photograph: Roadside ditch near Tyvan, Saskatchewan by Nora Stewart

Frontispiece watercolour: *Lilium philadephicum* by Jim Sullivan

Source of the quote on page 55 is: Home Place: Essays on Ecology (2002) by Stan Rowe. Reprinted by permission of NeWest Publishers Ltd.

The quote on page 101 is reprinted with permission from The Wheatgrass Mechanism. Copyright 1992, Don Gayton. Published by Fifth House Ltd., Calgary, Canada.

Nature Saskatchewan and the authors gratefully acknowledge the support for the production of this book as provided by Saskatoon Nature Society, Canadian Prairie Lily Society, Nature Regina, and Canadian Wildlife Service, Environment Canada. The book was financially assisted by the Saskatchewan Heritage Foundation, an agency of the Government of Saskatchewan. Nature Saskatchewan also acknowledges support from Saskatchewan Lotteries.

To order directly from the publisher, please add $4.50 (shipping and handling) to the price of the first copy and $2.00 to each additional copy to a maximum of $15. Send cheque or money order to:

Nature Saskatchewan
206 - 1860 Lorne St.
Regina, Saskatchewan
S4P 2L7

For information on more Nature Saskatchewan publications go to: www.naturesask.ca

TABLE OF CONTENTS

There is a Mohawk proverb that states, "The people do not make the land; it is the land that makes the people." In Saskatchewan, we are defined by our relationship with the land, the expansiveness of our sky, the kind of individualism that stems from surviving our strange dance with the elements, and the fact that in all of our 651,900 square kilometers, we number only one million residents.

Our provincial floral emblem, the Western Red Lily, symbolizes this fundamental connection. The wild lily continues to bloom, despite urbanization, cultivation, and drought. It is a metaphor of the survival of the First Nations and of the pioneers who chose to stay despite all of the challenges.

Anyone who has seen a red lily growing in the wild is captivated by its beauty. Is it possible that this miracle of nature has a practical purpose? This unique book sheds light on the mystery of our lily and its important role in the web of life. The pages that follow contain fascinating information in a readable and entertaining format, as well as more than 100 colourful images. But these chapters include much more.

The lily has become part of our collective identity, and is a prominent symbol on our provincial flag and Coat of Arms. It also has meaning for individuals. Bonnie Lawrence and Anna Leighton have included many personal stories that poignantly describe the significance of the wild lily in the lives of our people.

I applaud Nature Saskatchewan for publishing this tribute to our provincial flower during our Centennial. Our 100th birthday is a celebration of all that has made us who we are. The bold and resilient Western Red Lily is a magnificent part of the land that we love.

Dr. Lynda Haverstock
Lieutenant Governor
Province of Saskatchewan

PREFACE

Sometimes a tree, flower, animal or special place becomes inextricably entwined in one's life—a point of reference, an anchorage. So the prairie lily or 'tiger lily' is for my mother. Her birthday is the seventh of July, at the peak of bloom of the plant that became Saskatchewan's floral emblem, the Red Lily. She was born in 1916, when prairie agriculture was in its infancy—plowing the prairie had begun in the previous decade but there was still far more native prairie or pasture than field. Most roads were dirt trails and the land was abundant with sloughs, wild fowl, wild animals, mosquitos and wild flowers.

My mother did not have to walk far from home to find lilies flowering. They grew near a large slough in the pasture south of the barn and along the wagon trail that led to the nearest neighbour and family of similar-aged kids. Lilies grew in abundance.

On the seventh of July 1993, for her seventy-seventh birthday, my mother and I, with my children and cousin, embarked on an auspicious outing—back to where the lilies grew on my grandfather's farm. We set out with high hopes and a bountiful picnic lunch, in case our spirits couldn't sustain us. The slough in the pasture south of the barn was a dry depression and although we searched among the aspen that had appeared there since my mother's time, not a single lily stem could be found. We then followed the old wagon trail between a large freshwater pond and an alkali slough, and there we saw not just one, but hundreds. They grew in scattered drifts on all sides of the shallow slough. Many were tall stalks with multiple blooms waving like glorious banners and some were sprightly singles in a band amongst the cobble terrace close to shore. We had found a slough of lilies.

Questions immediately surfaced. Why had lilies disappeared from one part of the landscape while still so abundant in another? To answer that, I decided to tag individual plants along the slough margin to see what happens to each lily from one year to the next. The following year, I persuaded Anna Leighton, my botanist friend, to join me in a detailed study of lily populations and asked Dr. Taylor Steeves, Professor Emeritus at the University of Saskatchewan, for assistance in this pursuit. We set out two research plots on the Steeves' property south of Pike Lake and that fall began a study of the growth and plant structure. By good fortune, I participated in a fascinating plant walk led by Dean Nernberg, Grassland Ecologist with the Canadian Wildlife Service, in which he described some of the effects of controlled burning on native vegetation at Last Mountain Lake National Wildlife Area. In the summer of 1995, Anna and I began setting up study sites at the north end of Last Mountain Lake to examine the effect of fire and grazing on lily growth. Our methods of field study were simple: tagging, measuring and plotting the position of each individual lily plant. Over the next few years, we established a total of ten research plots in these three locations and annually monitored individual plants for eight to ten years. In 1995 we also began planting lilies raised from seeds or bulb scales into small field plots so we could follow a uniform population of known age.

For the last decade, our efforts to understand the secrets of this beautiful plant have meant the careful teasing out of its many relationships with soil organisms, insects, small mammals of the mouse, vole and gopher variety, and larger mammals, including humans. The lilies have become an important part of our lives. It has been a pleasure to get to know a little swatch of nature as well as we have. We join the many beings (be they two-, four- or six-footed) that have the lily as that special point of reference.

Bonnie J. Lawrence

A note about names

To avoid the confusion that arises from each plant having several common names, we have tried to be consistent with our use of common names throughout this book and, for each plant species that is named, we have given the scientific name equivalent in Appendix II.

In spite of this you may wonder (as we did when writing this book) what is the best name to use for the lily that this book is about. Unfortunately, there is no easy answer. We settled on the name 'Red Lily' for several reasons. This name has been in use in the province since the early 1900s. Is is broad enough to include lilies in both wooded regions as well as the grasslands where the name 'prairie lily' arose. It also includes all the wild lilies in the province, unlike the name 'western red lily,' which refers specifically to plants of the western variety. The varieties intergrade, making it difficult to distinguish between the two, and identification of varieties was not something we tried to do in our study. We have capitalized the name Red Lily so that is easy to recognize as the name of the plant and is not mistaken for an unidentified lily that is red.

"There is no more gorgeous sight in nature than a field of Red Lilies in bloom in early July. Even the chance glimpse of one or two along a roadside or among trees in open woods is a picture to enjoy."

Elizabeth Flock, *Wild Flowers of the Prairie Provinces*, 1942

George Jostn

A lasting impression

Saskatchewan's wild lily is the stuff of legend, story and mystery. Known locally by many names—prairie lily, tiger lily, western red lily, wood lily—it is referred to in this book simply as the Red Lily. We share this lovely plant with most of central North America, where it is greatly admired for its bold colours, erect and open posture and flamboyant spirit. A bright accent in a woodland glade, it is in the grassland setting where it can, and briefly does, explode into a flight of scarlet lilies.[1]

You may have heard recollections of family or friends seeing the prairie splashed red with this plant or experienced first-hand the flowers glowing with their intense and eye-catching colour. You may have wondered why you didn't see them in the same place every year or why they no longer appear where you saw them before. What makes them come and go? The plants seem akin to a troupe of actors with dramatic entrances and exits, sometimes standing up in a glorious chorus, more often popping up singly as if from some hidden stage door, and sometimes missing the scene altogether. Whatever the situation, their presence is always impressive and frequently memorable.

"The joy of coming on a lily in its native haunt is a particularly satisfying experience each time it happens." – Norma Pfeiffer, *A bouquet of thoughts on lilies*, 1960

A roadside encounter

Delving into the secrets of our wild lily

With many tantalizing questions and stories about this plant to investigate, we began a search for answers. Since our quest was to try to understand its behaviour, we began to study a portion of several populations. All the populations we studied are in the grassland area, but they represent quite different habitats: an upland meadow along the western bank of the South Saskatchewan River south of Pike Lake, a wetland margin of an alkali slough east of Saskatoon, and saline upland and moist meadow at the north end of Last Mountain Lake. Although many of our descriptions of the interactions of the lily with other plants, animals and weather reflect this bias toward the grassland prairie region, the lily is by no means only a prairie plant. In Saskatchewan it is most widely found in the Aspen Parkland region and extends its range north until the Canadian Shield reveals itself.

The Red Lily is protected in Saskatchewan as the floral emblem, not because it is rare or considered at risk. It is, however, rare in some other parts of its range and could become so in Saskatchewan with the deterioration of its native habitat. What can be done to ensure that this plant flourishes and not just

THE PROVINCIAL FLOWER AND THE PROVINCIAL BIRD

"Does any one know if it is a common practice of the Sharp-tailed Grouse to dig up the bulbs of the Red Lily?.... Last July Mr. Ritchie, [of Wallwort] came across some particularly fine Red Lilies, one of which had four blossoms on the one stem, so he placed three stakes by the plants, intending to come back and lift the bulbs later in the season. In the fall he went back and 'Imagine my disappointment,' he writes, 'on landing at the spot to find two of the bulbs scratched out of the ground. The third dry stock was still standing, so I dug the bulb up carefully, with plenty of soil attached, to transplant to my perennial bed. However, it was plain to see what had happened to the others. All around was evidence of the recent presence of the Sharp-tailed Grouse: their droppings and some stray feathers were lying all about. I investigated further and found other bulbs scratched up here and there. Is it possible that these birds have a liking for the Red Lily bulbs?'...As Mr. Carmichael remarked, 'Would it not be an irony of fate if one of our provincial emblems should destroy the other?' "
– Isabel Priestly, *Information please*, 1946

survives? Knowledge of its habits and favourite habitats enables us to do more than enjoy its beauty. Understanding its place and function in the living world is to gain a new appreciation for the stories it has to tell us about the world we share.

An emblem ought to mean something

A great deal of thought went into the selection of a floral emblem for Saskatchewan. The search for appropriate flower and bird emblems began in 1935 with an initiative launched by the Regina Natural History Society.[2] Some of the important factors considered were how widespread the plant was in the province, how common or likely to be seen, whether the plant had already been chosen by another jurisdiction and the need for protection. The western variety of *Lilium philadelphicum* became the floral emblem in 1941. (See Appendix 1)

"There was a time when the Red Lily bloomed in vast numbers everywhere. Then it began to decrease, partly due to the increased cultivation of the land. That was inevitable as people surged west....Red flowers are not very common and the very showiness of our lily has all but proved its undoing. When flowers decrease as the population increases, the smaller number of flowers must be left for a larger number of people to enjoy. Only through education and public sentiment can the Red Lily be saved." – Elizabeth Flock, *Wild Flowers of the Prairie Provinces*, 1942

Around this time, the provincial natural history societies began to invite comments about the perceived loss of wild flowers in general and the Red Lily in particular. It was not uncommon at the time to pick wildflowers; the brightness and beauty of the lily made it a frequent target. It was hoped that an education campaign would discourage people from picking lilies and encourage the setting aside of sanctuaries. In the mid-1940s, Dorothy Morrison wrote a book called *The Prairie Lily* for the schools and a survey of the province was carried out by encouraging citizens to send in information about the presence of lilies. Although many reports were positive, particularly in the Aspen Parkland region, the naturalist community was well aware that the prairies were changing and greater conservation efforts were needed. For the province's 75th anniversary in 1980, 'Leave a Legacy of Lilies' (a poster and information campaign) was launched and official protection for the Red Lily was sought. In 1981, the lily became a protected species where it grew on public lands. For the Saskatchewan Natural History Society (Nature Saskatchewan), the Red Lily became a symbol for the need to conserve the diminishing wild places.

Viola Coutu

A symbol to share

What does the wild lily mean to people? Bold Spirit, Courage, Peerless Beauty, Wildness, Wilderness? To Dorothy Morrison, who first posed the question in her book, *The Prairie Lily*, the glowing red of the lily was like the bold spirit of the pioneer. The meaning of the lily is as worthy of consideration today as it was in 1948. What does the lily mean in the scheme of life? There is many a story to share.

"As a child less than three years old, I experienced the newly-opened prairie lands, and I can recall the pastures of virgin grasses. Each July the prairies were red with our native *Lilium philadelphicum*, and invariably each year I was reprimanded for having the rusty red pollen of that lily all over my nose, spread there as I smelled the unique perfume of its flowers." – Jean Ericksen, *My adventures with lilies*, 1979

"This flower was very special to me. It was not common in our area where I grew up. When I married in 1953, my late husband, when he came home with the milk cows, would always come home with a lily for me. This was a tradition he did once a year for 'his gal,' as he put it. For a few years they weren't so plentiful, but now seem to have made a comeback. Now my grandchildren won't pick a flower. They come in and say 'Grandma, we saw the lilies.' These lilies are so special at our house, thanks to my late husband, who introduced them to me." – Mrs. Ruth Rosom, survey participant, McLean, 2000

"While still quite young, around six years of age, I recall being shown my first 'wood lilies.' I had never seen anything but *Opuntia polyacantha* [Plains Prickly-pear] blooms, roadside Buffalo Beans (*Thermopsis rhombifolia*), tiny, sticky wild blue asters and in general, unprepossessing wild flowers. The wonder of that first colony of *L. philadelphicum* is as vivid today as it was then [50 years ago]. It was at a point where the foothills to the mountains began and the prairie grasses became mixed deciduous, but scattered copses. There, within one hundred yards of the old gravel highway was a large patch of lilies. I was awed by them. Each flower seemed so large, so perfect and had such deep red/orange color and such big black spots. I remember Dad saying not to pick any. I would not have done so anyway, for I had an intense reverence for what I was seeing....*L. philadelphicum* is of infinite value to the traveler, who may turn a corner someday and catch sight of a truly vivid, wild beauty." – Eugene Fox, *Growing to understand Lilium philadelphicum*, 1993

"Tiger Lilies have always fascinated me. My birthday, July 5, was always recognized with a walk in my grandparents' pasture in search of these red-orange beauties. Now that I'm married and a recent grandma, I hope to do the same with my granddaughter someday." – Shirley Becker, survey participant, Sonningdale, 2000

Shirley Johnston

12

Part 1
KNOWING THE LILY

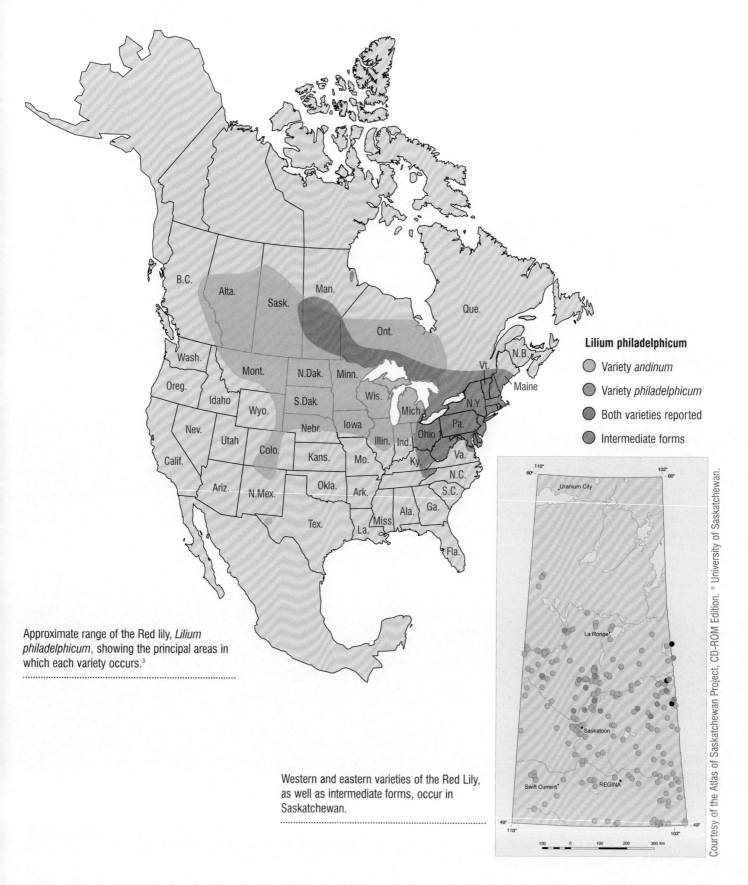

Lilium philadelphicum

- ○ Variety *andinum*
- ○ Variety *philadelphicum*
- ● Both varieties reported
- ● Intermediate forms

Approximate range of the Red lily, *Lilium philadelphicum*, showing the principal areas in which each variety occurs.[3]

Western and eastern varieties of the Red Lily, as well as intermediate forms, occur in Saskatchewan.

14

CHAPTER 1

What you see

One plant with many names

"It is so bright in colour that it has been known by numerous vernacular names such as the 'Flame lily,' 'Wood lily,' 'Wild orange lily,' 'Orange cup lily,' 'Red lily,' 'Glade lily,' and 'Huckleberry lily.' " – Patrick Synge, *Lilies*, 1980

In this book we refer to Saskatchewan's wild lily as Red Lily, although in Saskatchewan it is also called prairie lily, western red lily and tiger lily. Name it what you will, there is only one wild lily species in the province. Designated the floral emblem of Saskatchewan in 1941, it grows throughout the province north to the Precambrian Shield.

The western variety, *andinum*

The eastern variety, *philadelphicum*

Jim Sullivan

The scientific name of Saskatchewan's wild lily is *Lilium philadelphicum* and although there is only one species, there are two varieties. The variety that grows primarily in western North America, variety *andinum*, is often called 'western red lily' to distinguish it from the eastern variety *philadelphicum*, often referred to as 'wood lily.' Although both varieties grow in Saskatchewan, only the western one is widespread here. The eastern variety edges into the province along the Manitoba border. Intermediate forms between the eastern and western varieties have been reported from central Saskatchewan as far west as Brightsand Lake.

WHAT'S IN A NAME?

Lilium philadelphicum was first named by Carolus Linnaeus (the famous Swedish taxonomist) in 1762 from specimens sent by John Bartram, a botanist/farmer from the Philadelphia area. Linnaeus gave its habitat as 'Canada.' With the subsequent exploration of western North America, botanists initially thought the western form to be a separate species and gave it the names *L. umbellatum* (Pursh, 1814) for the umbellate or umbrella arrangement of the flowers and *L. montanum* (A. Nelson, 1899) for its type location in the Rocky Mountains of Wyoming.[4] The varietal epithet 'andinum' was originally assigned as a species epithet by botanist Thomas Nuttall, who encountered the western red lily near Fort Mandan in North Dakota in 1811.[5] Nuttall believed that the plant occurred west to the Rocky Mountains. He considered these to be a northward extension of the Andes, so he named it 'andinum,' meaning 'of the Andes.' *Lilium philadelphicum* var. *andinum* is the variety designation in use today.

15

Red, orange or red-orange?

Despite the name 'Red Lily,' the flowers are seldom truly red. Orange-red lily, an earlier common name for this species, better reflects the typical flower colour. This species, however, is well known for its colour variation, and does not confine itself to red-orange. It has playfully unleashed its pallet, giving us petals of shocking red, salmon, red-orange, muted orange and yellow, all washed with yellow at the base and splashed with purple spots.

George Tosh

Bouquet of five flowers on one stem

Reports of unusual colour variations are legion in Saskatchewan. "Mr. Sidney F. Tinkner, field officer with the Department of Natural Resources at Prairie River reports that last summer [1947] he discovered a fine specimen of the Red Lily....it was a bright yellow, with a pinkish heart." [6]

C. S. Francis reported from Torch River in 1950 that his son Stanley found a wild lily which was "at least two feet tall, with two very large blooms, of unusual beauty. The petals were of a bright red on the outer edge, gradually turning to an orange or a highly strong yellow, while the spots in the throat, which are usually almost black, were of a beautiful clear lilac color. It was strikingly different from the others that were blooming all around it." [7]

The most unusual colour form has unspotted yellow petals. Lacking red or orange pigment, flowers of this form are usually described as 'lemon yellow,' but also as 'pure yellow,' as no spots mar the yellow cup—even the anthers and stigma are yellow like the petals. The distinctive yellow colour form is referred to as forma *immaculatum*, meaning 'spotless' in Latin. Hugh Raup assigned the name in 1934 based on a specimen from Jenkins Lake, Alberta. [8]

One flower, two flowers, three flowers, more

Although usually one-flowered, lilies with two to four flowers are not uncommon. Rare plants with five and six flowers make their own bouquet. Plants with seven flowers are even more rare. We photographed seven flowers in a head, all mostly devoured by insects, in the Last Mountain Lake National Wildlife Area on July 6, 1997. Another seven-flowered plant was reported by W. N. Craig of Massachusetts, who "found as many as 7 [flowers] to a stalk, though under cultivation he could not obtain more than 5 to a stem." [9]

Observations of eight, nine and ten flowers per stem come from Saskatchewan residents: "eight perfect blooms on one stem" in the wet years of the early 1940s, [10] the plant with nine flowers described by Charles Thacker of

Broadview (below) and a "Prairie Lily with nine flowers and one bud" reported by Mrs. Oliver Olafson of Tantallon.[11]

"While out for a drive early in July, Mrs. Thacker and I observed what appeared to be a large ball-shaped red flower. We turned around and went back to investigate. It turned out to be a clump of Red Lilies, *all on one stem.* From one side of the group to the other measured seven inches one way and six inches the other. The entire group made almost a perfect circle....The one stalk at the top measured one quarter of an inch each way and was roughly rectangular shaped, but the stalk had five distinct ridges in it, as if five stalks grew in one." [12]

Why some plants produce stems with more than one flower when most have single flowers relates to environmental conditions and the genetic makeup and age of the plant. In a plant's first flowering year when the bulb is small, only one flower will appear; it takes several good growing seasons to build up a sufficiently large bulb to produce a plant with multiple flowers. Optimal

Jim Sullivan

THE CHALICE AND THE TRUMPET

The upward-facing flower—a chalice open to the sky—is one of the most striking features of our lily. Among North American native lilies, only the pine lily (*Lilium catesbaei*) of the southeastern United States has a similar flower. The rest face downward or outward. Red Lily flowers that face outward are occasionally found as noted by Jim Sullivan: "While looking at hundreds, perhaps thousands, of these lilies during a recent summer, I found a population with some stems with out-facing flowers. This unusual conformation led lily enthusiast and grower, Wilbert Ronald, to exclaim, 'Aha! Hardy trumpets on the Prairies.'" [13]

conditions of moisture and nutrient availability at the time when plants form their flower buds for the next year may lead to an increase in the number of flowers per stem. Many plants, however, continue to produce single flowers year after year even under good growing conditions.

Lily plants that produce more than one flower per stem do not always increase their number of flowers from one year to the next. In exceptionally good growing years, they may add a flower or two, but in poor years, or if there has been some drain on bulb reserves, the number of flowers can stay the same or drop. We have seen lilies jump from a single flower to three blooms (and from two flowers to four) in response to good growing conditions. We have also seen a plant with three flowers in a moist year reappear with a single flower in the following year after a dry spring.

Jim Sullivan

Jim Sullivan

Shirley Johnston

"Red lilies in prime, single upright fiery flowers, their throats how splendidly and *variously* spotted,

18

John Kozial

hardly two of quite the same hue and not two spotted alike...."

Henry David Thoreau, journal entry, July 12, 1856.[14]

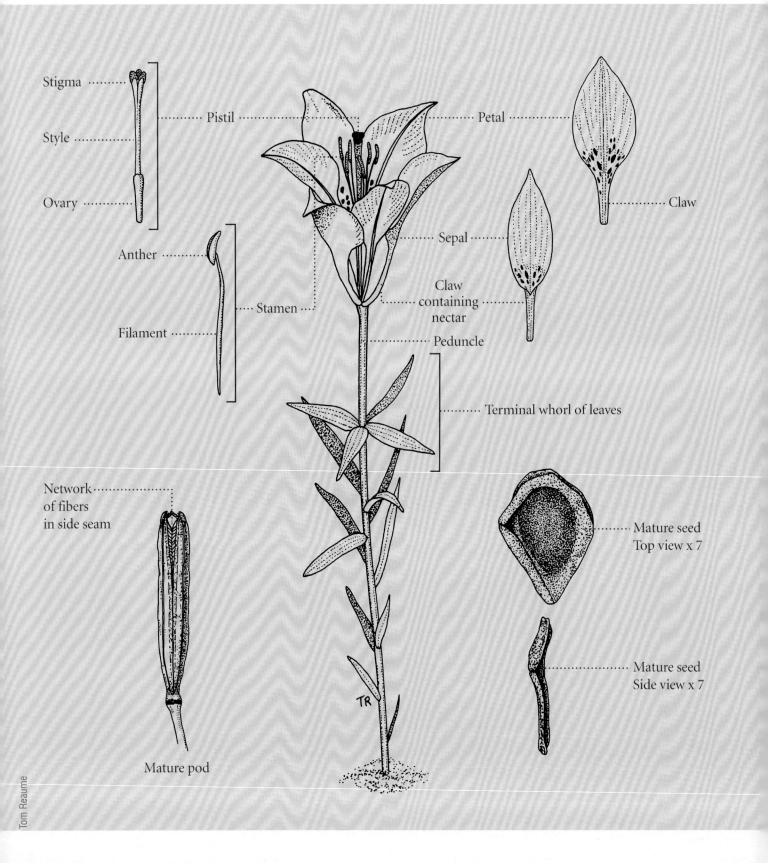

Stigma

Style

Ovary

Pistil

Petal

Claw

Sepal

Anther

Claw
containing
nectar

Stamen

Filament

Peduncle

Terminal whorl of leaves

Network
of fibers
in side seam

Mature seed
Top view x 7

Mature seed
Side view x 7

Mature pod

TR

Trios and sextets: the lily flower close up

Lilies hardly need to be introduced; most of us cannot recall a time when we couldn't recognize a lily. A close look, however, reveals details missed when we admire them for their colourful flowers.

Typical of lilies, the Red Lily has flower parts in threes or multiples of three: three sepals, three petals, six anthers, a three-lobed stigma and a three-chambered ovary and pod. Oddities do occur. A Red Lily flower shown in Appendix IV displays parts in multiples of four: four sepals, four petals, eight anthers and a four-lobed stigma.

The sepals and petals, being brightly—and similarly—coloured, look like six petals but in fact form two series and differ in shape. The narrower, longer-tipped sepals alternate with the broader, rounder petals. Not only are the petals wider than the sepals, but they have two parallel ridges plainly visible down the middle of the topside of the petal. On the underside of each petal, there is a light-coloured ridge—the only part of the petal visible in the closed bud.

Variation in shape of petals (top) and sepals (bottom) from three different flowers.

Both petals and sepals taper abruptly to a narrow base called a claw, but only on the sepals do the edges of the claw curl inward to form a hollow tunnel. It is within these tunnels that nectar is produced. Insects can reach the nectar from the bottom or top since the tunnel is open at both ends. (The entrance to the tunnel is visible as you look down into the flower.) The curled part of the claw varies in length depending on the size of the sepal; in some plants it measures just over 1 cm, in others it reaches 2 cm.

Each stamen consists of an anther (the producer and dispenser of pollen) and a filament (the slender stalk that supports the anther), and each arises at the base of a petal or sepal. The anther hangs vertically from the filament tip, attached to the anther near the middle of the side facing the pistil. When touched, the anther rocks like a teeter-totter between the petal or sepal and the stigma, touching neither.

The claws are curled on the two sepals (bottom) and flat on the petal (top). An ant has found the nectar in the sepal claw.

The lone object in the centre of the flower is the pistil, with the ovary (where the seeds are produced) at its base, the stigma on top and the style in between. The stigma, the part of the flower that receives pollen, stands at anther height or just a little taller. When a pollen grain lands on the stigma, the grain sends a tube down through the style to reach and fertilize an egg inside an ovule. Ovules are housed in the ovary and, when fertilized, develop into seeds.

Canadian Tiger Swallowtail probing the nectary at the base of a sepal.

The tips of the swallowtail's wings brush against the anthers as the butterfly moves from nectary to nectary.

Who pollinates the lily?

To set seed, Red Lilies require pollen from another plant.[15] How this pollen is transferred remains something of a mystery to us, for after ten years of observing flowering lilies, we have seen pollination take place at only a few locations.

Red Lily flowers open toward the sky, with spreading petals that offer large butterflies the landing platform they require. Swallowtails, Great Spangled Fritillaries and Monarchs are considered to be the principal pollinators of this species.[16] The flowers also have several attributes attractive to hummingbirds: red, showy petals and nectar stored in narrow tubes. However, upward-facing flowers are thought to be awkward for hummingbirds, which approach flowers from the side and prefer those that face down or sideways.[17]

In Saskatchewan, the only insect we have observed pollinating Red Lily flowers is the Canadian Tiger Swallowtail. These large butterflies transfer pollen on the underside of their wings. After landing on a flower, they visit the nectary at the base of each sepal. While doing this, their large wings touch the anthers causing them to brush their full length against the wing surface. The stamens, which bend away from the pistil, probably prevent the wings from touching the stigma during this manoeuvre, but when the butterfly lands on the next lily flower, the underside of the wing may hit the stigmatic surface.

Northern Crescent basking on a lily petal.

The lilies that we observed being pollinated by swallowtails were growing in two locations: a shrubby hillside in Aspen Parkland and a grassy knoll in the boreal forest. Aspen poplar, a common host plant for Canadian Tiger Swallowtail caterpillars, was growing near the lily plants at both locations. Spreading dogbane was blooming among the Red Lilies at these sites and the swallowtails visited flowers of both plants for nectar.

Results from a Wisconsin study indicate that the presence of companion plants, such as spreading dogbane, that attract butterflies, may increase the rate of pollination in the lilies present. A compact, vigorous, ditch-side population of Michigan lilies growing around a mailbox in an otherwise mowed area set seed in only 10 % of the flowers. "A population several hundred yards down the road in a non-mowed ditch with a variety of companion plants set seeds on all blossoms."[18]

Resident swallowtails pollinate the Red Lily across its range. The only other upward-facing lily in North America, the pine lily in the southeastern United States, is also pollinated by swallowtails: primarily the Palamedes Swallowtail and, to a lesser extent, the Spicebush Swallowtail.[19]

A nectar-seeking large fritillary (*Speyeria* species) deep in a lily flower, with wing tips barely reaching the anthers.

Other insects visit the Red Lily in Saskatchewan to take pollen or nectar, but, with the exception of large fritillaries (butterflies of the genus *Speyeria*), their smaller size or behaviour would appear to prevent them from being effective pollinators. The motley assortment of nectar-robbers and pollen-eaters that we have observed includes crescent butterflies (members of the genus *Phyciodes*), various ants, an 8-mm long bee, another small bee taking pollen while crawling on the anthers and three immature bush katydids. A study in Michigan found that sweat bees (*Dialictus* spp.), in addition to Monarchs, Great Spangled Fritillaries and Eastern Tiger Swallowtails, pollinated Red Lilies.[20]

This immature Broad-winged Bush Katydid (*Scudderia pistillata* Brunner) is enjoying a protein packed meal of lily pollen. We have seen this occasional visitor to lily flowers, with its remarkably long hind legs and antennae, in only two years: 1994 and 2004.

The anther, a re-closable sack of pollen

When mature, each lily anther consists of two long sacks joined along their inside seams and suspended vertically from the tip of a filament. When the flower first opens, the sacks are closed. On exposure to warm, dry air, each sack splits vertically along its outside seam and the walls fold back to expose the pollen-coated interiors.

The anther's job is to deliver pollen to potential pollinators. With an ability to rock its pollen-coated exterior back and forth at the top of the filament, the anther can brush pollen against anything that touches it.

Flowers that face skyward, like Red Lilies, present anthers with a unique problem: they expose them to rain. In flowers that face down or outward, petals and sepals shelter the anthers, reducing the risk of rain washing off the pollen or getting it wet. Moisture can damage pollen or cause it to germinate before it is transferred. Red Lily anthers have a built-in mechanism for closing when it rains, an adaptation not found in many flowers. Just as drying stimulates the anthers to split open, moisture causes them to reverse the process.[21] After about 15 minutes of light rain, the anthers begin to close and under conditions of steady rain, they close completely. Closing protects the pollen. On drying, the anthers re-open, making pollen available for insects that fly when the sun is shining.

Each anther balances at the tip of a filament. In this photograph, taken at the end of a rainy morning, the anthers are still closed from the rain. They are also horizontal, something we have seen only under wet conditions.

Anthers closed in response to rain.

Anthers open on the same flower, photographed several hours after the rain had stopped.

Flower bud about two weeks before opening.

Coloured flower bud starting to open.

This flower has just opened and the anthers, still closed, crowd around the stigma.

Flickering flame

Catching a lily in flower is like watching a fire burst into flame before it goes out: a brief moment of brilliant visibility between the unseen bud and the hidden pod. It's not that the flowers are short lived—on the contrary, each lasts a week to ten days—but that there is only one flower, or very few, per plant. The lily is unusual in this regard. Most of our familiar prairie wild flowers produce a series of blossoms, with new flowers replacing the faded ones over a period of days.

The flower buds begin to colour about ten days before the flowers open. Stem growth ceases around this time but the peduncle (the stalk that supports each flower) continues to lengthen as the flowers open and even after the petals drop. By the time the petals and sepals turn orange, the bud is open at the bottom, in and around the narrow claws.

Three sepals enclose the bud. The only part of the petals visible is the pale green midrib running vertically between the sepals. At the top of the bud, red and white hairs on the underside of the sepals press against those on the upper side of the petal tips, effectively sealing the top of the flower. As the sepal tips pull apart slightly in advance of opening, a hole opens up between the hairy tips and one can look through the interior of the bud to the spaces created by the claws at the bottom of the flower.

The flower is fully open and the anthers have split lengthwise exposing reddish-brown pollen.

A flower whose spent petals are about to drop. The anthers have withered but the pistil is still attached.

An ovary developing into a seed pod. The pistil has fallen off and the ovary is plump. The chalky, oval patches at the base of the ovary are scars showing where the petals and sepals were attached.

Flowers open early in the day—the petals spread and the anthers bend away from the pistil before splitting lengthwise to expose the pollen. If a flower first opens on a warm, still morning, a faint but distinct fragrance lingers in the chalice.

The petals remain open regardless of the pollination status of the flower[22] and drop about six to nine days after opening. When the petals fall, the ovary is revealed and, if there has been fertilization, the ovary will develop into a seed pod.

Pod invisibility

Only flowering lilies catch our eye. A patch of lilies is easily found when blooms are present, yet after petal drop, the plants seem to disappear. The pod develops virtually unnoticed; at first it is green like the surrounding vegetation and then it turns brown in synchrony with the plants around it. In Saskatchewan, the pod grows into a plump, green cylinder during July and August. The pod turns brown and starts to crack open along the side seams sometime in September, depending on the year and the individual plant.

The seeds, stacked like dinner plates in six piles inside the pod, can exit when the top of the pod opens. A network of fibres, left in place as the side seams separate, blocks the passage of seed out the sides. Not free to fall to the ground at the base of the plant, the seeds are jettisoned out the top when the pod is jostled. The pods do not empty right away. Seeds that fall onto packed snow in winter scud across the surface, pushed by the wind to the edges of bluffs or into hollows where snow collects.

"Somewhat surprisingly, given its relatively modest stature, the wood lily [Red Lily] has the longest capsules of any *Lilium* in North America."[23]

As shown in a series of pods collected in 1996, below, Red Lily pod (or capsule) size and shape vary considerably in any given year. The pods range from heavy and long, like pod 3 at 0.92 g and 5.3 cm, to light and short, like pod 10 at 0.10 g and 2.3 cm. The number of seeds varies considerably also: four pods (3, 4, 5 and 6) contained over 300 mature seeds, (pod 4 had the greatest number at 371) but pod 10 contained only 17, along with 194 undeveloped seeds. Pods 1, 8, 9 and 11 each had over 250 mature seeds.

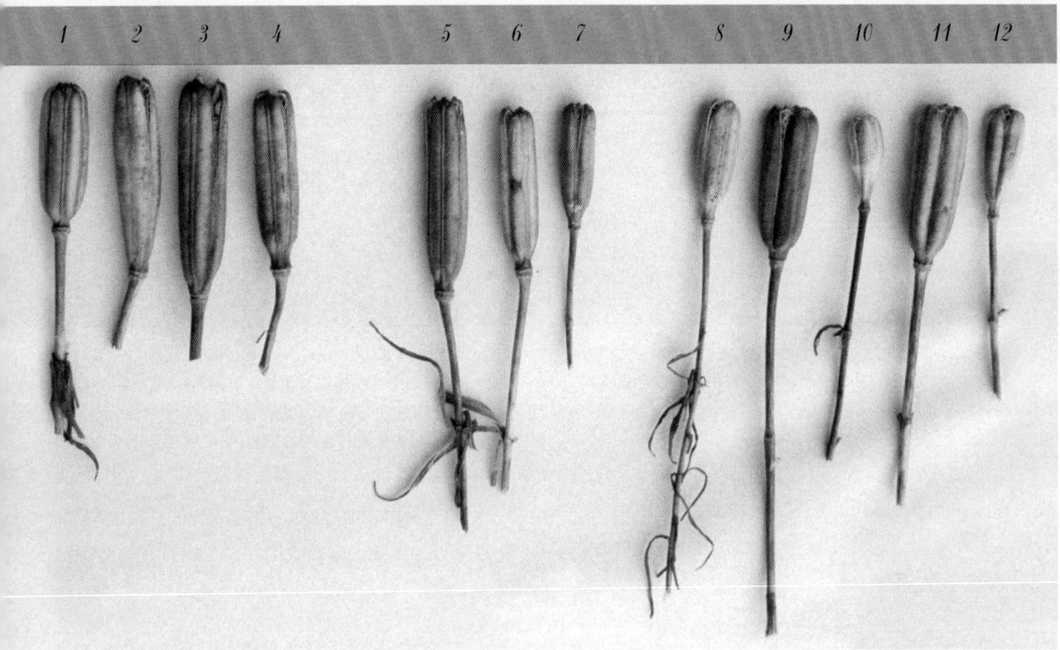

Twelve pods collected from one location in late September 1996. This series shows the natural variability in pod size and shape.

Shape may reflect the amount of seed development in the pod. Pods that taper at the bottom (pods 2, 10 and 12) contained more undeveloped seeds than mature seeds. Pods roughly cylindrical in shape contained mostly mature seeds.

All but two of the pods shown above are from single-flowered plants; pod 3 is from a two-flowered plant and pod 2 is one of five pods produced by a five-flowered plant. Although pod 2 is large and its seeds are among the largest produced by the pods sampled (5.5 mm in diameter), it contained only 144 mature seeds along with 280 undeveloped seeds. One possible explanation for the large number of undeveloped seeds is that flowers on plants with multiple flowers may receive significant amounts of pollen from other flowers on the same plant, resulting in a large proportion of unfertilized ovules. Pod 3, on the other hand, contained 325 mature seeds and only 53 undeveloped ones. Perhaps the pollinators landed on this flower first when coming from a different plant, bringing pollen for cross-fertilization.

The plants that don't flower

The non-flowering forms that grow among the flowering lilies must be looked for or go unseen. With their green stems and narrow, almost grass-like leaves, non-flowering lily plants blend in with the surrounding vegetation to a remarkable degree. While lilies with multiple flowers often grow above the plants around them, and single flowers usually open at the height of the rest of the vegetation, the non-flowering forms stay below the canopy.

One non-flowering form that occurs regularly in lily populations is the vegetative plant produced in the years before (and often after) the lily reaches the flowering stage. Vegetative plants have upright stems, some delicate, some robust, which in our studies have ranged in height from several centimetres to over 20 cm, but are usually in the range of 7 to 10 cm high. Vegetative plants generally break through the ground in spring before the shoots of flowering lilies and may shrivel up by midsummer.

Less common than vegetative plants, but often found, are lilies with one or more flower buds that fail to develop. We call these 'plants with aborted buds.'

A large vegetative plant, 23 cm in height, photographed in August. The long, narrow leaves are typical of vegetative plants.

Like flowering plants, they have a leafy stalk ending in a terminal whorl but flower development is interrupted when they are in bud so they never flower. Instead of a flower, they have a pale bud that can range in size from a tiny nubbin only 1 mm long to a 1-2 cm long bud that superficially looks like a flower bud. Lilies may abort flower development in a number of circumstances. The two we have identified are hot, dry, spring weather (as in April 2001) and after a late spring frost (as in the third week in June 2004).

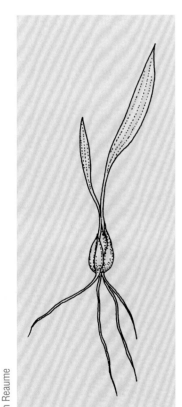

Tom Reaume

Two strap-shaped leaves growing from a young bulb composed of a few simple scales.

In addition to the stalked plants, lilies produce single leaves that arise directly from the bulb. A series of oval leaves, several centimetres long, is produced from the young bulb in the first season of growth. Larger leaves, shown at left, up to 10 cm in length and broadly strap-shaped, grow from the bulb starting in its second season of growth. They also occasionally show up on well-established plants as a low-cost method of building up the bulb reserves through photosynthesis.

An aborted bud plant with a pale bud about 1 cm in length.

29

Two plants with the soil cut away to reveal their bulb beneath the surface. The robust plant (left) with four flowers measures 44 cm from the bottom of the bulb to the tip of the petals. The delicate, single-flowered plant (right) is 30 cm from the bottom of the bulb to the petal tips. The base of the bulb on the right is 4 cm below the surface and the base of the bulb on the left is about 4.5 cm.

What you don't see

The lily bulb

The lily plant arises from a bulb located just below the soil surface. If the lily is the flame, the bulb is the fuel. As the only part of the plant that persists from year to year, the bulb acts as the bank and the powerhouse; it sends up the new growth in spring and stores the summer's surplus for the next growing season. The bulb also plays a role in propagation: if broken apart into its component scales, it can reproduce itself many times, like the bewitched broom of the sorcerer's apprentice.

If you were to push your thumb into the ground, its tip would reach the bottom of most lily bulbs. Mature bulbs sit between 3 to 5 cm below the surface with the base typically at 5 cm. Bulbs of large flowering plants, such as the plant with four flowers (opposite) are, roughly speaking, the size of a small walnut and can be as tall as 2 cm or even a bit taller. Those of smaller plants, such as vegetative plants or those that produce only single flowers, are closer to filberts in size.

Fleshy scales that resemble rice grains make up the bulk of the bulb. Roughly 1 cm long, the scales are starch-filled and white with a concave inner surface for close packing over other scales. The scales form a cluster around each shoot that develops on the bulb. The bulb of a large mature flowering lily will contain several dozen scales; a smaller plant, about two dozen. The scales toward the outside of the bulb usually consist of two parts (occasionally three) joined by a constriction in the middle. These 'jointed scales,' (referred to as 'wasp-waisted' by Woodcock and Stern[24]) occur only in a small number of North American lily species. The scales toward the centre of each cluster are oval in shape, and lacking the constriction, are referred to as 'simple scales.'

There are two kinds of roots that grow from the bulb: thin, branched roots that take up water and nutrients, and fatter roots that pull the bulb down into the soil. The latter, called contractile roots, are a common feature of bulb-bearing monocots like the lily, allowing plants that start growth on the surface to pull themselves to the proper depth for life as a mature plant. How these roots actually work is poorly known, but they are recognized by a layer of wrinkled outer skin, like that of an elephant's trunk. In addition to the roots that grow from the bulb, stem roots grow just below the soil surface on the stems of robust flowering plants.

At the centre of the bulb is the basal plate described in Woodstock and Stern as "a solid basal mass (*axis* or *basal plate*), i.e. an extremely short stem, on which the bulb scales are mounted. This central axis is the most important part of the bulb since it produces the roots, the scales and the buds for new growth."[26] Despite its small size, the basal plate gives rise to all the scales, the shoots and the roots of the lily plant. The basal plate is visible only when all the scales are removed.

(Top) Mature Red Lily bulb in early summer cut in half vertically to show the attachment of scales to the basal plate and the position of the flower stalk. To the left of the flower stalk is the cluster of scales surrounding last year's shoot. To the right is a small growing point that will become next year's shoot.

(Bottom) The same bulb, viewed from the top, cut horizontally just above the basal plate. The bases of the current and past year's flower stalks are shown in cross-section and the position of the developing shoot is visible to the right of the current shoot.

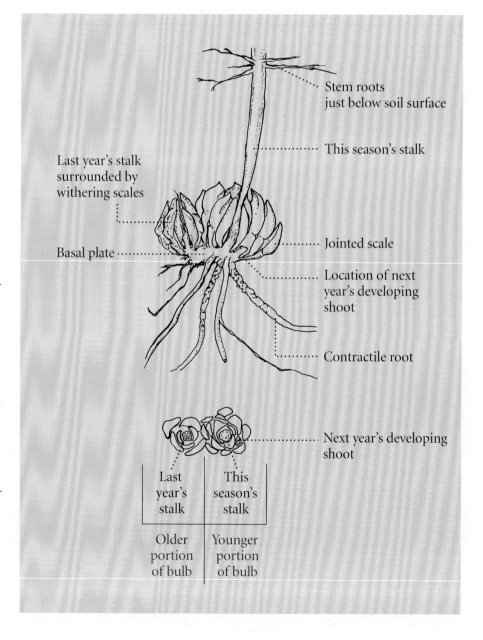

Stem roots just below soil surface

This season's stalk

Last year's stalk surrounded by withering scales

Jointed scale

Basal plate

Location of next year's developing shoot

Contractile root

Next year's developing shoot

Last year's stalk

This season's stalk

Older portion of bulb

Younger portion of bulb

LILY BULB THRIPS

The presence of Lily Bulb Thrips (*Liothrips vaneeckei* Priesner) dramatically affects the regulation of growth in the lily bulb. These small (2.5 mm) gregarious insects use their mouth parts to pierce and rasp the inner surface of the bulb scales. The intact bulb (shown below) changes in response to this damage; abnormal structures, such as the finger-like growths on the right, are initiated from the basal plate. Over several seasons, the bulb breaks apart, leaving groups of growing scales interspersed with dead and dying tissue. The presence on the soil surface of 20 strap-shaped leaves at one location indicated a disintegrated bulb whose parts are shown in the photo below.

Lily Bulb Thrips. The light tan insect on the left is immature (a second instar); the larger, darker one is an adult.

Adult Lily Bulb Thrip beside the old, brown stem base within the scales of a lily bulb.

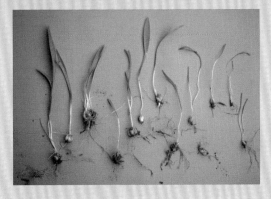

The dissected remains of a bulb that fragmented after being fed on by Lily Bulb Thrips in 2004. In 1999, the lily was an 18 cm tall vegetative plant.

Grandmother-Mother-Daughter: seasonal changes within a bulb

The layout of the bulb changes during the growing season as scales appear and disappear on different parts of the bulb in response to shifting demands. We begin the story in spring, keeping in mind that following the changes within a bulb is like observing an escalator: as one step appears, another disappears.

Early spring bulb and flower shoot before the scales were removed as shown at right.

The bulb in spring has two clusters of scales, snuggled together at the base. One cluster has a ragged brown stalk emerging from the centre, surrounded by scales that are beginning to turn grey and lose their plumpness. This is the grandmother cluster and she is beginning to shrivel. Beside her is the mother cluster, the picture of vitality, with plump, pearly-white scales. Emerging from the centre of the mother cluster is the elongating shoot stretching up to the soil surface. Completely unseen close to the base of this emerging shoot is a tiny growing point, so small that it can be seen only by using a microscope. By mid-June this bump will be a flat raised mound, about the size of a pin head, covered with encircling flaps of tissue that resemble miniature leaves. This is the beginning of the daughter cluster.

Midsummer bulb with base of flower stalk visible.

Throughout the growing season, the mother cluster dominates the bulb. To one side, grandmother gradually disappears as her scales wither and diminish in number. On the other side, the new daughter cluster is developing. The tissue of the shared basal plate has extended like a lip to support this new up-and-comer. By flowering time, the scales of the daughter cluster are about half the size of a fully developed scale and envelop the shoot that will emerge in a subsequent year. For the next few months, the bulb consists of three clusters of scales.

Late fall bulb with base of flower stalk visible.

The bulb in the late fall again has only two clusters. Grandmother has disappeared as the daughter cluster was growing. The mother cluster has reached middle age. Her scales are still plump and large. In the outer ring of scales, the joints are only loosely attached. If some local disturbance should happen, the top portion of these scales would break off to take on a life of their own. By the next spring the mother cluster will become the 'grandmother.' The daughter cluster has a full complement of scales. Growth will continue until frigid soil temperatures halt the process. The shoot within the daughter cluster is now about 1 cm long and recognizable as a miniature stalk with flower petals already formed and completely enclosed in layer after layer of tiny leaves. Cell division continues late into the fall in preparation for rapid spring growth.

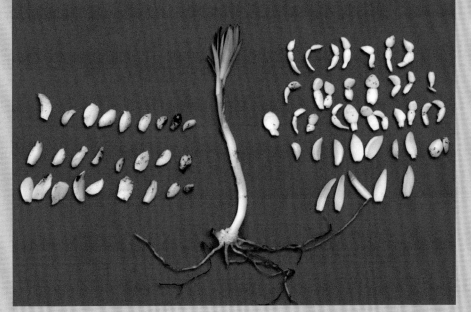

Scales from a bulb in early spring. The mother cluster scales are on the right, grandmother cluster scales, on the left. Outside scales are at the top of each series; inside scales, at the bottom. Note the jointed scales from the outside of the mother cluster. The brown base of last year's shoot is just left of the base of the current flower shoot.

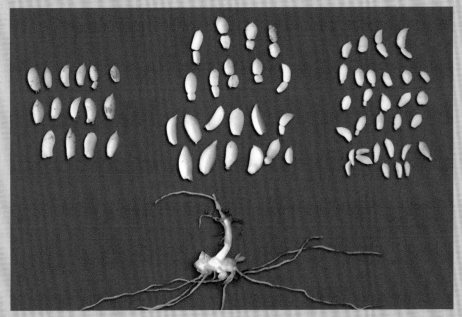

Scales from a bulb in midsummer. Daughter cluster scales are on the right, mother cluster scales in the centre and grandmother scales, on the left. The developing daughter shoot is visible as a tuft of small scales to the right of the broken off flower stalk (centre). Last year's stalk was located in the mound on the left.

Scales from a bulb in late fall. Daughter cluster scales (right) are almost as large as the mother cluster scales (left), and about half are jointed. The grandmother cluster no longer exists. The daughter cluster produced the tall white shoot on the right. A brown base is all that remains of the shoot from the mother cluster.

In late May, the emerging shoot of the mature bulb with two bulb clusters elongates towards the soil surface (horizontal line). The small bulb, situated closer to the surface than the mature bulb, has already sent up a strap-shaped leaf.

In mid-June, the green flower bud is cradled in the terminal whorl of leaves. The stem below the whorl is fully elongated, stem roots are beginning to grow at the soil surface and the scale cluster around this stem is larger than the older cluster on the right, which is beginning to diminish.

In early July, the flower has just opened, the stigma is able to receive pollen and the stem roots continue to develop and anchor the plant. The new daughter cluster is visible near the base of the flower stalk.

By August, the ovary has grown into a green pod on an elongate stalk. The lower stem leaves are beginning to wither although the stem, upper leaves and peduncle remain green. Within the bulb, the daughter cluster has grown to nearly full size and the cluster of the previous year has withered.

In October, all above ground structures have turned brown. The capsule has opened from the top and is splitting along the seams. The seeds within the capsule are mature and ready to be shed. Within the bulb, scales around next year's shoot have enlarged and the new shoot is obvious as a sharp point above the cluster. New roots have developed at the base of the daughter cluster. The small bulb has a green strap-shaped leaf that is beginning to wither and turn yellow. Its bulb has become more open and the outer simple scales have taken on the appearance of jointed scales.

Stages of growth

The progression of bulb growth from a seed to a stalked plant is a fairly orderly affair with a lot of flexibility in timing.

The first true leaves follow the emergence of the grass-like cotyledon. Oval in shape and lasting an average of four to six weeks, these leaves mark the position of a new bulb. Not all the leaves arise simultaneously, for they are the green extensions of little scales that start as a slightly enlarged leaf base. As the leaf manufactures food that is then transported downwards, this basal portion plumps up, taking on the shape and appearance of a small scale. This process continues with each scale swelling from products of its leaf blade and some additional scales growing from the minute basal plate as food is stored away. The roots begin to pull the young bulb, the size of a pea, deeper.

By the next growing season, the larger strap-shaped leaves emerge from the bulb. Like the first true leaves, a series of several strap-shaped leaves typically emerges throughout the growing season. A bulb that is regularly producing strap-shaped leaves is slightly taller than it is wide and composed of less than a dozen simple scales. If growing conditions permit, the bulb will make a transition at the end of the growing season to one that can produce a stalk.

The first stalk is typically vegetative with less than a dozen leaves on its stem. It is common to find a strap-shaped leaf growing with the first stalk. The bulb, now the size of a dime, has a few jointed scales on the periphery. The fall bulb is composed of two scale clusters with the daughter cluster often positioned lower in the soil, giving the entire bulb a downward slant. At this point the bulb has reached a stage of maturity with the typical succession of bulb clusters, as outlined in grandmother-mother-daughter above, each with its own stalk. Large bulbs, however, in some situations, may initiate more than one growing point. This is a process known as 'twinning' in other species of *Lilium* and is a means of increasing the number of stalks and ultimately forming two separate lily bulbs where there was one.[27]

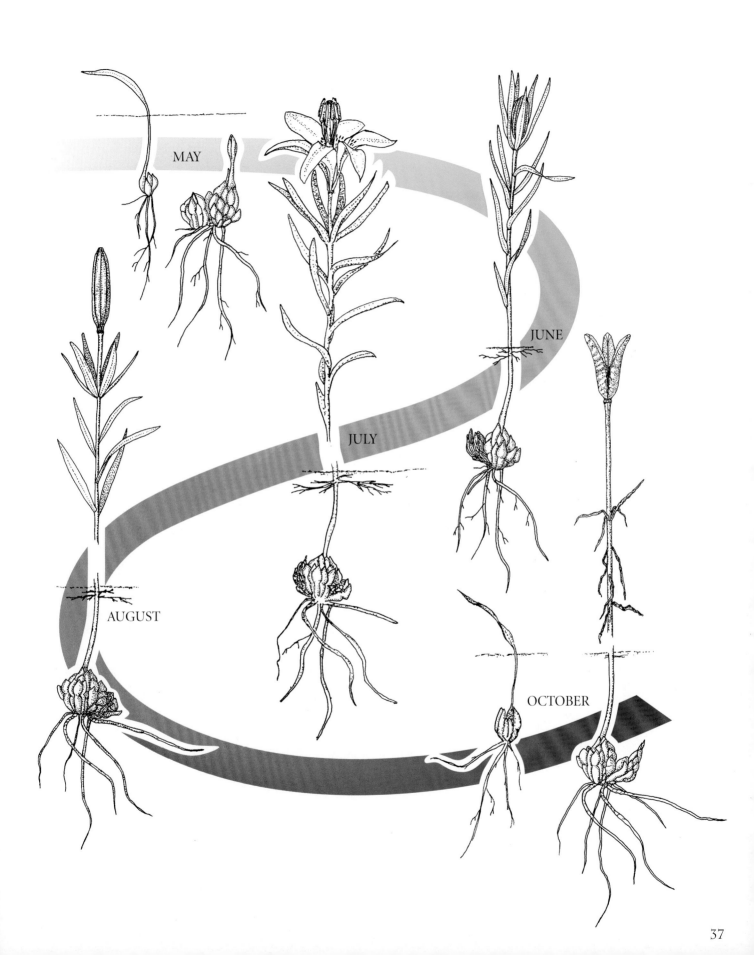

MAY

JUNE

JULY

AUGUST

OCTOBER

37

From each scale a new plant grows

The appearance and disappearance of scales during the course of the growing season demonstrate the important nutritive role played by the scales; their potential to produce new plants becomes evident only after the scales are removed from the parent bulb.

A bulblet growing from the base of a bulb scale (lying horizontally) has a green leaf and four roots. The wrinkled surface of the large root on the left indicates that it is a contractile root.

When detached from the bulb, every scale and each part of the jointed scales have the ability to produce a new plant. We have found that there are two potential growth areas on the inside edge of the base of each scale and each portion of the jointed scales. When the scale is placed in soil, a bulblet (the beginning of the new plant) starts to grow on this part of the scale. A root then appears, followed by small scales. Starting at about five weeks after planting, the first leaf, with an oval blade about 1 cm long, appears above the surface.

The ability to grow a plant from each scale may be useful to gardeners who want to increase the number of plants from one parent bulb, but how does it serve the wild plant growing under natural conditions? Because the scales are not released to grow until removed from the parent bulb, they become propagules only when the bulb is broken apart or disintegrates, or if individual scales get separated from the parent bulb. All these things can happen in nature. Hooves of grazers penetrate the soil and break up roots of all kinds, including lily bulbs. Thrips feeding on bulb scales can also lead to disintegration of the bulb. Voles, mice and pocket gophers, which dig up bulbs for food, unwittingly leave some of the peripheral scales behind, especially parts of jointed scales which break off easily in fall.

These independent scales are often deep in the ground. Those with sufficient reserves can send a large strap-shaped leaf to the surface to build up the bulb reserves with the products of photosynthesis. Those growing from small or depauperate scales can advance toward the surface with a ladder-like growth of one new scale above another, forming an ascending chain of scales.

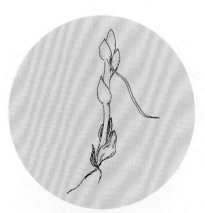

A chain of small scales growing toward the soil surface from several withered scales.

Scales have several advantages over seeds when it comes to establishment: they contain a reserve of starch, they begin life within the soil (rather than on top) where the moisture supply is more dependable and, being a genetic copy of the parent plant, they should be able to survive at that particular site. Seeds, which contain new combinations of genetic material, are the principal colonizers of new ground.

Part 2
PRAIRIE SURVIVOR

CHAPTER 3

A plant with dense hairs, Indian breadroot.

A plant with bitter, milky sap, Skeletonweed.

Dean Nernberg, CWS

A plant with spines, Prickly-pear cactus.

Unarmed and edible

Unarmed and edible

Imagine a survival strategy that allows for being eaten by an inefficient diner. Superficially it seems terribly flawed. It is easy to understand the presence of prickles and thorns to deter a plant eater, or the fuzziness of many hairs that would detract from the dining experience, or better yet, the presence of some bitter or toxic chemical that would bring quick avoidance. The lily doesn't have any of these characteristics. The leaves, stems and flowers, lacking protective hairs, have a vibrant glossy appearance. For many plants of the prairie, such hairs have a dual function of reducing palatability and minimizing water loss. The lily is completely unarmed and edible.

The prairie environment abounds with plant eaters—numerous insects whose populations rise and fall with favourable or adverse conditions; the large hoofed animals such as deer, antelope and, at one time, bison; a multitude of small mammals: mice, voles, pocket gophers, ground squirrels and hares. Over the years that we have been observing lilies, some prairie diners have appeared with the emergence of the new lily shoots in the spring, some with the growth of the flower buds, others with the development of the ovary or seed pod and a few in the fall, when only the seed stalk and the over-wintering bulb are present. Each appears in its own time.

The voracious caterpillars

Leaf rollers: The first insects observed on newly emerging lilies belong to a group of small moths, the leaf rollers or tortricids. The caterpillar's ability to spin silk enables it to tie leaves together to form a temporary feeding shelter. Protected from weather and predators by its own little tent, it dines in safety until it literally eats itself out of house and home and must find the next suitable plant in which to set up camp.

Petal and sepal bases, parts of filaments and the lower part of the ovary are all that remain after caterpillar feeding.

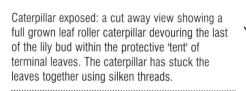

Caterpillar exposed: a cut away view showing a full grown leaf roller caterpillar devouring the last of the lily bud within the protective 'tent' of terminal leaves. The caterpillar has stuck the leaves together using silken threads.

Caterpillar tent opened to reveal leaf roller caterpillar lying along the margin of the leaf to the right. Note white patches of webbing and the brown spot—all that remains of the top of lily stalk eaten by the caterpillar.

Several species of leaf rollers find lily plants suitable. When lilies first emerge in May, the leaves enclose the tip of the plant. As the stem elongates, the leaves unfurl from the bottom up. At this stage, the first species of leaf roller, *Sparganothis xanthoides* (Walker), is present. Its feeding tents look just like an emerging shoot. Only a biologist, determined to discover whether or not there is a tiny bud inside the growing shoot, would disturb this hidden diner and send the caterpillar to the ground as it quickly lowers itself on an instantly-spun silk thread. The full grown caterpillar is about as long as a nickel is wide but in the process of maturing it outgrows its skin several times and daily consumes more than its weight in leaves and buds. It will emerge as an adult in early July, about the time the lilies bloom.

Several other species complete the caterpillar feeding stage when the lilies are in bloom. The most common is the Sparganothis Fruitworm Moth larva, *Sparganothis sulfureana* (Clemens). These insects consume some flower buds and leaves near the top of the plant, thereby reducing the possible seed production, but they do not consume enough of the plant to be detrimental to the persistence of the lily bulb. In most years only a small proportion of the lily population is affected by leaf rollers but occasionally conditions that favour insect populations reign and many lilies will have served as home and entrée for these insects.

Tiger Moths: We first encountered the remnants of a tiger moth's dinner when photographing a seven-flowered lily (opposite page, bottom right). It was in tatters. Since that year, we have found and photographed this very hungry caterpillar, the Dubious Tiger Moth, *Spilosoma dubia* (Walker), in action. The members of the tiger moth family (Arctiidae) are admired for their beautifully patterned and often colourful wings. Some tiger moth caterpillars are called 'woolly bears' in reference to their large size and abundant hairs or bristles.

The remains of a lily stalk, photographed on 12 July 2001, with the leaves and top chewed off by an insect. This plant, which first flowered in 1999, must have had substantial bulb reserves, for even though the flower stalk was chewed off three years in a row (2001, 2002 and 2003) it sent up a stalk with four flowers in 2004.

Dubious Tiger Moth caterpillar feeding on a lily bud through a hole it chewed at the base.

The Dubious Tiger Moth adult (female shown) emerges in spring.

A mature cutworm, belonging to the moth family Noctuidae, is gulping down a hearty meal of seeds after chewing a neat hole near the top of the pod.

A lily plant with two flowers chewed to the base by an insect, possibly a tiger moth caterpillar. The two brown spots visible at the top of the stem are the remains of the individual flower stalks. The leaves were left intact and continue to photosynthesize, providing the plant with food reserves for the future.

Red Lily plant with seven flowers eaten by a caterpillar.

43

Dubious Tiger Moth caterpillars eat leaves, but appear to prefer flowers, whether open or in bud. Typically they approach a flower from the bottom and chew in from the side, consuming inner flower parts as well as petals. When numerous, and when the period of caterpillar growth coincides with lily flowering, these caterpillars reduce seed production by destroying flowers, but probably have little impact on the bulb reserves or the flowering potential for the following year.

A mature caterpillar can make quick work of a lily bud. One individual raised during its final larval stage ate, in less than two weeks, 114 lily leaves and a complete flower, as well as some garden columbine and chokecherry leaves when the lily supply ran out. It is fortunate that this species has only one generation a year, overwintering as a pupa and emerging as a nectar-seeking adult in the spring.

Nipped in the bud

Who can resist the plump sweet treat of a fully formed lily bud glowing with colour and ready to open? Deer can't. We learned of this predilection the day after we saw an unusual lily plant with five out-facing buds just about to open. Determined to get a photo of this oddity we returned the following morning to see a flowering stalk without any flowers. The lily, located along a path frequented by deer, was a pleasant appetizer to the deer and a missed opportunity for the photographer. Since that time we have frequently seen neatly nipped flower stalks, leaving all the leaves to continue to manufacture food for the plant. It is possible that some of the nipping in the bud is the result of hares but our most common sightings in the study sites have been deer.

Deer target the flower buds, whereas cattle and bison are less discriminating grazers. Their impact is on a habitat scale, whereas deer have an impact at the population level by reducing the number of lily flowers. In areas of high deer populations, such as Wisconsin, there is concern that over-browsing may adversely affect seed set among Red Lily populations.[28]

Red Lily with five out-facing buds photographed before the connoisseur visited.

Mouse-root

The Cree named the Red Lily 'Appecooseesh-ootchoepeh,' meaning Mouse-root "because the common mouse of the country, a species of Campagnol, feeds upon its scaly bulbs."[29] The name speaks directly to the important relationship between the lily and the 'mice,' also known as voles, that store the lily bulb for food.

The English common name 'vole' comes from the Norwegian word *vollmus*, meaning field mouse. Voles are secretive creatures with blunt noses, round ears, short legs and short tails. They trot-scurry rather than hop, are largely vegetarian and rarely enter human habitation. Though as common, they are less conspicuous than the smaller but more familiar deer mouse, which has a sharp nose, beady eyes, erect ears and long tail.

Two species of vole, the meadow vole and the prairie vole, collect and store large winter caches of plant tubers, roots and bulbs, whatever is abundant in their area. Other small mammals, such as deer mice and red-backed voles may also harvest bulbs. Vole caches were utilized by various North American peoples as a handy pre-sorted food source. "Indian women gathered grain, beans and rhizomes by the bushel from the 'bean mouse' caches."[30]

Voles do more than dig and cache lily bulbs for winter food stores. In midsummer, they chew down the stalks, leaving piles of matchstick-sized stem pieces, and in the process harvest the green swelling seed pods or green leafy stems. They also eat the green shoots in the late spring during years when these small mammals are very numerous. Vole populations, particularly those of the prolific meadow vole, go through cyclical highs and lows approximately every three to four years.[31] In some years, such as fall 1996-summer 1997, the vole population explodes with an echoing increase in birds of prey and mammalian predators. The population crash after the 1997 'vole high' was made evident by an almost complete absence of chewing in our research plots the following year.

Once a lily stalk is chewed off, the plant does not send up another shoot that year. Due to the storage nature of the bulb, the plant can withstand at least three successive years of chewing, even if this occurs before the flowering season, and still send up a stalk the following year.

One of the most interesting features of the Red Lily bulb, the scales, enables the lily to reap a benefit from vole harvesting. *Lilium philadelphicum* is one of the few North American lilies that have jointed or segmented scales on the periphery of the mature bulb. On some particularly large bulbs there can be three segments to a scale and each segment is capable of becoming a new plant. These outer scales become loosely connected to the basal plate and to adjoining segments as they age. In the fall it is difficult to extract the entire

THE BEAN MOUSE

The meadow vole's habit of hoarding 'beans' of the hog peanut plant (*Amphicarpa falcata*) earned it the name 'bean mouse.' Plains peoples—Omaha, Ponca, Pawnee and Dakota—who valued the beans as food, let the voles do the tiresome work of gathering them from pods that grow scattered along underground branches.[32]

People appreciated the efforts of these small mammals, considered to be "very industrious" by the Omaha and helpful to human beings, so they left food in exchange for what they took.

".... The women of the Dakota nation....said it was their custom to carry a bag of corn with them when they went to look for the stores of beans gathered by the animals, and when they took out any beans, they put in place of them an equal quantity of corn. They say that sometimes instead of corn they put some other form of food acceptable to the animals in place of the beans which they took away. They said it would be wicked to steal from the animals, but they thought that a fair exchange was not robbery."[33]

bulb without loosening the outer scales. The vole, in the process of digging the bulb, litters the digging site and leaves scales along its route of travel.

In the decade of studying lily populations, we have encountered many small pits in our research plots. We noted the first of these holes in the fall of the year we planted some one-year-old plants. A third of our new plants had been extracted, leaving an empty pit where each pea-sized bulb had been. These plants never grew again. This suggests that, unlike jointed scales, the small simple scales of immature bulbs are not spread when handled by voles.

Several years later at a different planting site we again observed pits where plants had been. This time the digging occurred in a research plot fenced to exclude cattle, which had, as a result, higher, denser vegetation than the surrounding area. There was clear evidence of well travelled vole runways into the planting area. Three-quarters of the bulbs in this planting site had been dug. However, the plants were five years old at the time of digging and many had produced stalks with leaves and bulbs with jointed scales. The pits were correspondingly deeper. One to two years after the vole harvesting, we began to see lilies reappear at a quarter of the pit locations.

"To breed like Rabbits is an old measure of fecundity.... These mice [Microtus spp] can mate, multiply and raise to independent age a whole family before the Rabbits get much beyond the period of gestation."

Ironically, our efforts to protect the planting site from trampling by cows created a wonderfully safe habitat for the voles, as the fence also excluded foxes and coyotes. The voles' canopied runways encircled the fence like a racing oval with little side paths leading to the planting site and our 3 m by 4 m research plot. We should have known it would not take the voles long to turn their attention there. They excavated 11 pits at the base of our copper tags that marked the positions of the lilies. Imagine our surprise upon also finding small pits started at the opposite end of plant tags lying flat along the ground. Clearly our tags were signs for voles, saying "DIG HERE FOR MOUSE-ROOT." A year or so later, many strap-shaped lily leaves were noticed scattered in the area, indicating new bulb growth. Another plot in the vicinity now has distinct, deep pits at a fifth of the tags. Humbled by this example of rodent learning we sincerely hope they won't share the meaning of copper tags with voles in the other locations where we have research plots.

In a pocket gopher's garden

As chance would have it, one of our research plots became part of a pocket gopher's home territory shortly after we established the plot. A pocket gopher's average home range is 120 to 160 square metres.[34] Our 3 m by 4 m research plot was only one-tenth of this size and was situated on the edge of the territory. In July 1993, we marked seven flowering lilies in the area. When we returned in the spring of 1994, the area had been extensively disturbed. There was no sign of the plants marked in 1993 other than some old seed stalks but there were nine new flowering lilies. In June 1995, there were 31 lilies with flower buds, but by July the majority either had been chewed or had mysteriously disappeared. Harvesting of lily plants had begun in late June in the portion of the research plot near some shrubs and had continued like a wave throughout the plot.

A gardener's tools: sharp, chisel teeth that grow at a rate of over 3 cm per year; teeth that protrude in front of lips to allow cutting of roots without getting a mouthful of soil; large, external cheek pouches extending to its shoulders; long claws and strong forearms.

On the positive side, the numbers of new plants tagged each year in this research plot was amazing. Ten years after we began observing this area we had tagged 183 stalked plants or an average of 15 per square metre. This was without doubt our most prolific research plot. A spadeful of soil dug close to the plot contained five lily bulbs large enough to have a stalked plant and several small clusters of a few scales. On average the bulbs were 3 to 5 cm apart. The most obvious explanation for the proliferation of lily bulbs was that a pocket gopher's churning of the soil during the extensive surface tunnelling had broken apart existing bulbs and had distributed scales and parts of bulbs throughout the area. The pocket gopher seemed to concentrate on harvesting the leafy portions of the plants above the ground or pulling down plants into its shallow feeding tunnels.

By the following year (1996), either this individual had died or was tunnelling elsewhere as only mouse holes were evident in the old mounds. The plot didn't experience the surface tunnelling again until 2002, when presumably a new 'gardener' came to disturb the soil and begin the cycle again.

In an adjacent planting area, we lost a quarter of the young lily plants to pocket gopher activity in the fall. We also had tagged plants 'disappear without a trace.' The ability of the pocket gopher to pull a large plant down into its feeding burrow beneath the plant was illustrated when it chose a plant that had a mesh bag placed around the flower as part of a pollination study. The force of the pull was sufficient that the bag was found crumpled into the soil with only some flower parts remaining inside.

"The one deterrent [to growing garden lilies] was and still is these wretched pocket gophers! Here they run underground and eat up hundreds of my best bulbs. Some persons call these animals moles, but they are not."

Jean Ericksen, *My adventures with lilies*, 1979

PORTRAIT OF A MEADOW VOLE
(*Microtus pennsylvanicus*)

The meadow vole, a heavy set, medium-sized field mouse is said to be capable of multiplying itself by six every six weeks. Females mature by the age of 25 days at which time they mate. After a gestation period of 20-21 days, the litter of four to eight young is born and the female can immediately mate again. The young are weaned at 12 days and the mother remains with them for another week, protecting them from wandering male voles. At the age of three weeks, the young are left in the nest and the mother goes off to make another nest for her next litter that is due to be born. In general, breeding starts in April with the first green vegetation and continues until October. Should she survive the season, the female could potentially have eight or nine litters—a continuous cycle of nest-making, giving birth and eating. In reality, the average life span is about two months. These voles are the base of the food chain for birds (hawks, owls, crows, shrikes, herons and cranes); mammals (weasels, skunks, badgers and foxes); snakes (garter and rattle) and even predatory fish that catch them as they swim and dive in water.

A meadow vole's nest is a bulky, globular ball of loosely woven grass and sedge, about the size of a flattened grapefruit and lined with plant down or finely shredded plant material. In wet areas, it is situated in a tussock of grass; in drier locations, in a natural hollow or an abandoned burrow. Winter nests are on the ground under the snow. Meadow voles are active year-round and store whatever seeds, underground roots and bulbs are locally abundant. They also chew the basal parts of grass beneath the snow and will strip bark from roots, stems and twigs if food is scarce. Being small animals with a high metabolic demand, they need a lot of food. In spring they feed on tender growing shoots and in summer they cut plant stalks into pieces to reach more succulent leaves and seed heads.

Meadow voles require habitats with ample grassy vegetation, such as abandoned fields, moist prairies, wetland margins and edges or openings in woods. Vole highways, a maze of criss-crossing paths, are easy to see if one parts the grass canopy. These tunnels through the grass are constructed by gnawing off grass stems and then tramping down the paths. Although meadow voles form extensive loose colonies that share runways, communal toilet and refuse heaps, and winter stores, they are by nature socially aggressive and scrappy.[35]

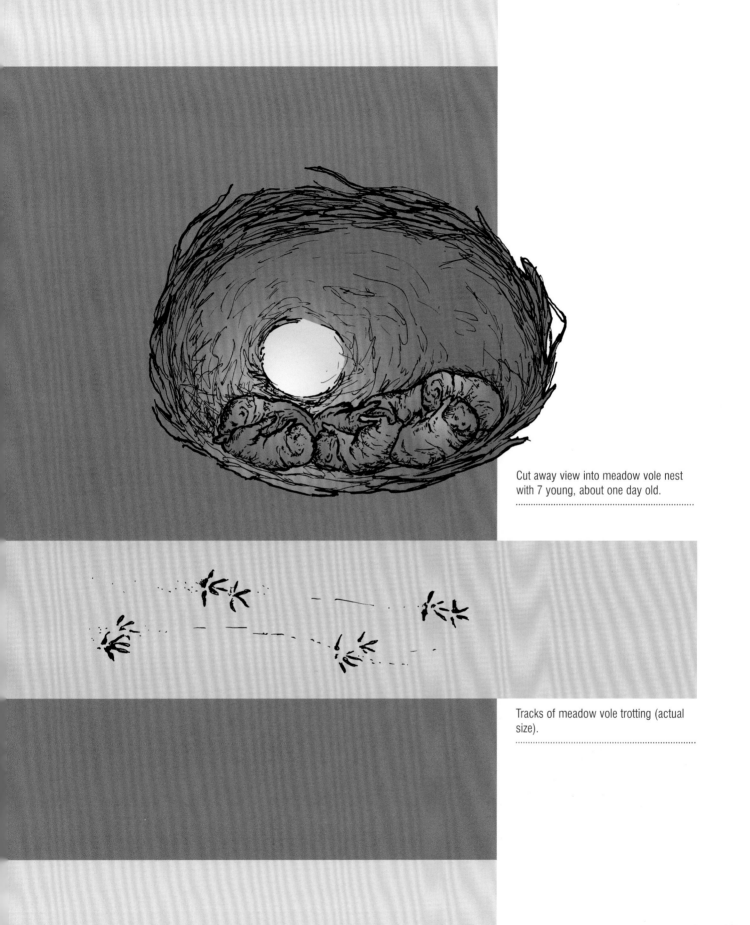

Cut away view into meadow vole nest with 7 young, about one day old.

Tracks of meadow vole trotting (actual size).

PORTRAIT OF A PRAIRIE VOLE
(*Microtus ochrogaster*)

An earlier name for this species was *Microtus minor*. In appearance it is a slightly smaller version of the meadow vole. It is also less numerous than the meadow vole. It takes longer to reach maturity, has a shorter breeding season (late April to September) and has fewer young per litter than the meadow vole. However, the loss of its traditional habitat, native upland prairie, is the greatest reason for this vole becoming less common than it once was.

Prairie voles can also be found in grassy areas along fence lines, in abandoned fields and at the edges of grain fields. Unlike meadow voles, they avoid wet areas and are not particularly bothered by mowing or burning. Their choice of homes, their tunnel building habits and their stable social structures would be adaptive for grazing and fire conditions in a harsh prairie environment.

A little grassy knoll, abandoned pocket gopher mound or abandoned anthill makes a preferred home. Such a mound may be honeycombed with little holes from which the animal's runways wind away through the grass. Burrow entrances are clean cut and drop nearly straight down. Old pocket gopher mounds are favoured as nurseries. Prairie voles build and maintain an intricate network of surface runways and subsurface runways to get from a burrow to a food source. By constant use and some digging, scratching and gnawing, the runways soon become tiny ruts. In some cases the majority of paths are underground tunnels, 5 to 10 cm beneath the soil surface. Often pocket gopher tunnels are utilized.

This colonial and socially tolerant animal forms stable colonies of up to nine individuals, beginning in September when winter preparations start and lasting until dispersal in late April. The winter nest is a melon-sized, underground chamber situated well below the tunnels and can be at least three times as deep. Soil, taken from the chambers, is often placed in a pile above the nest chamber to form a noticeable mound. The nest is lined with shredded grass or sedge and has several exits, presumably for escape if the nest is invaded by a least weasel. Tunnels link the nest chamber to the underground food cache located 25 to 50 cm away. The winter stores can contain an amazing 10 kilograms of whatever plant material is most abundant in the area: roots and bulbs (wild onion, sunflower, goldenrod, blazing star, lily, crocus, dandelion, psoralea, prairie sage), berries and galls (juniper), seed heads (wheat, dandelion, ragweed) and favoured grass clippings (bluestem). Summer food consists entirely of green plant material, with broad-leaved plants favoured above grasses and grass-like plants.[36]

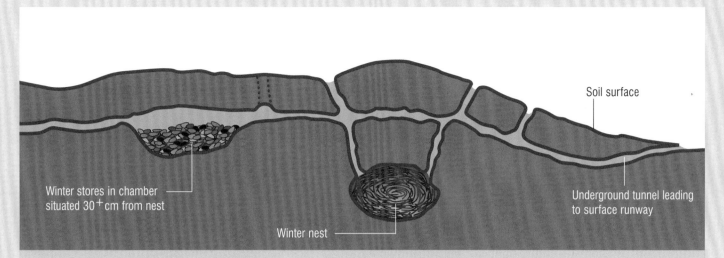

Soil surface

Winter stores in chamber situated 30⁺ cm from nest

Winter nest

Underground tunnel leading to surface runway

SCHEMATIC CROSS-SECTION THROUGH A WINTER HOME OF SEVERAL PRAIRIE VOLES:
The communal underground nest is well-lined with shredded plant material. Most of the intricate underground passages lead to the store room to which there is no direct entrance from above. (After Criddle 1926)

THE PRAIRIE VOLE AND THE PRAIRIE LILY

In 1947, Stuart Criddle described a food cache of the prairie vole in his article '*Microtus minor* [Prairie Vole] and Prairie Lily.'[37] "In a short article, 'Habits of *Microtus minor* in Manitoba,' *Journal of Mammalogy*, Vol. 7, No.3, 1926, I described a number of their winter stores. Since then I have examined a good many more. Perhaps the most interesting of which was one dug out on the 4th of November, 1945. While holding a decided personal interest, it is of some general importance as it shows how the Red Lily, wild onion and prairie anemone are greatly reduced in numbers in a short space of time by these mice.

"In 1944 I found two bright yellow lilies, a rare sport of *Lilium philadelphicum*. These I self-pollinated and procured their seed that fall. Hoping to get more seed in 1945, I left the bulbs where they were. Unfortunately deer, who are very fond of lily buds, found and ate them off just as they were about to burst into bloom. This made me decide to get the bulbs to plant in my garden, but when I went to do so I found that they had already been removed by these *Microtus*. After a short examination I found one of their main runways and followed it to their home sixty-three yards away. This was typically *Microtus* as all the earth excavated from the nest chamber and store room had been placed over the former and the store room itself made well away from the nest. Both were large which indicates that they had been made by more mice than the three caught by me.

"The store room was only about a third full of what appeared to be lily bulbs. However this was not the case, as when the contents were sorted out and counted, I found it to be composed of the following: 1176 lily bulbs (*Lilium philadelphicum*); 678 wild onion bulbs (*Allium stellatum*); 583 pieces of the rhizomes of sunflower (*Helianthus rigidus*); 417 buds and pieces of the taproot of pasque flower (*Pulsatilla ludoviciana*); and a few bits each of the red cedar (*Juniperus horizontalis*), avens (*Geum* sp.), sagebrush (*Artemisia* sp.), goldenrod (*Solidago* sp.), and prairie clover (*Petalostemon* sp.). Their respective weights, in grammes, were lily 2081, Allium 258, sunflower 123, pasque-flower 163, and the remainder 23, thus bringing the total weight to 2648 grammes."

This quintessential digging mammal has a number of amazing adaptations. The large, external fur-lined pockets which extend from its nose to its shoulders are used to carry plant roots and bulbs it finds in the process of churning through the soil. The quickly growing front teeth are used to nip roots, loosen soil and chew through almost anything in its path, including telephone cables. This thickset, sturdy animal has strong, oversized forefeet with long, sharp cutting claws; a broad head with small eyes and short conical ears, and loose skin with soft, silky dense fur that sheds the dirt. The telltale signs of pocket gopher activity are the mounds of loose soil it pushes to the surface by using its forearms like a bulldozer.

Robert E. Gehlert

The tunnels can reach to depths of over three metres, although most tunnels are shallow. Winter nests are on average two metres deep; summer nests are less than a metre deep. In spring, during the peak tunnelling season, a pocket gopher can dig at the rate of 50 metres per day, pushing up an average of three earthen mounds. The home proper includes deep tunnels, several small storage chambers and nearby spring and winter nests that are lined with finely-shredded plant material. When hungry, the gopher can slip out of its cozy nest, pad into the nearby pantry and bring back food. It appears that pocket gophers are fond of eating in bed. In all other ways they are described as neat and orderly animals.

In the spring and summer they forage at night above ground, cutting off plants close to the surface and pulling them back to their tunnels where they are cut into 5 cm sections, packed into their pockets and carried to storage chambers that hold up to 2 kilograms of food. After all the tunnels, summer nests and fresh food stores are ready, the mating season begins (from early May to early June). This is the only time this very solitary animal allows another adult into its burrow. There is only one litter (on average three young), which stays with the mother for six to eight weeks. Summer food consists of 70% leaves and 30% roots of plants such as "dandelion, peavine, artemisia, clover, anemone, goldenrod, yarrow and penstemon." Little digging is done in the summer unless cover is scanty; then the gophers tunnel just under the surface, harvesting food by cutting roots and drawing plants down. Fall is again a time of deep tunneling and preparation of a new winter nest and stores.

Pocket gophers occupy the same territory for their lifetime of approximately three years, although the area of tunnelling may change with the season. They will often extend their tunnels into recently dried marsh and pond edges, suggesting the animal's place of activity is influenced by the water table. Pocket gopher mounds are important habitat for mice and voles, as well as beetles, tiger salamanders and a wealth of hibernating fauna that seek the loosened soil.[38]

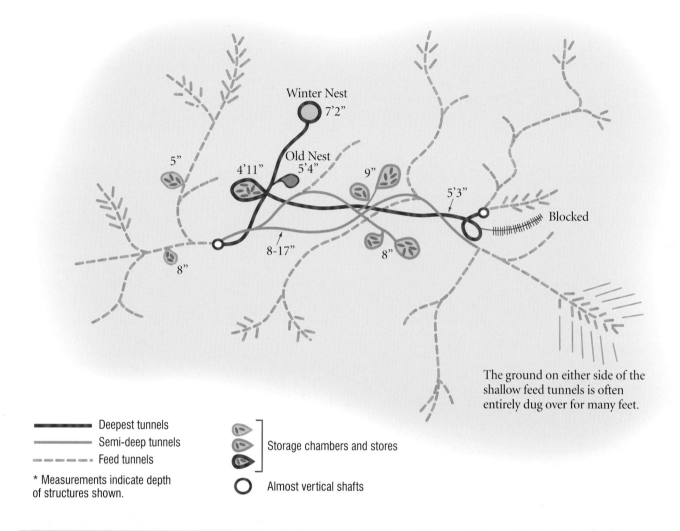

Winter Nest
7'2"

5"

4'11"

Old Nest
5'4"

9"

5'3"

Blocked

8-17"

8"

8"

The ground on either side of the
shallow feed tunnels is often
entirely dug over for many feet.

—————— Deepest tunnels

—————— Semi-deep tunnels

– – – – · Feed tunnels

* Measurements indicate depth
of structures shown.

] Storage chambers and stores

◯ Almost vertical shafts

MAP OF A POCKET GOPHER'S HOME

"Home No. 4. October 23 and 24, 1928. Locality sandy plain on virgin prairie. From the neatness of this residence, one might be led to believe that the owner was artistically inclined. The home was a new one and the work had all been done within about three months. A few of the first tunnels dug had been filled in with earth brought up from the deeper ones. This is a common practice which often makes it almost impossible to tell, by the mounds of earth thrown out, in what part of the tunnel system the home proper is situated. It will be seen that the nest was at the end of the deepest tunnel seven feet two inches down. This deepest tunnel and the remains of a small one, five feet four inches down, that had evidently been in use while the home was under construction, were the only ones in the home. The stores were somewhat unusually placed, two small ones well out on the feed tunnels, four larger ones towards the center of the home about nine inches down and another at the end of one of the deep tunnels four feet eleven inches down; these seven stores were all well filled....Thirty-three feet of deep tunnels, and thirty-seven feet of semi-deep ones from eight to seventeen inches down, composed the home proper. The two hundred and seventy feet of feed tunnels showed that a great deal of work had been done along their margins by the animal in following the lateral roots of *Commandra*." – Stuart Criddle, *The Prairie Pocket Gopher*, 1930

CHAPTER 4

Saskatchewan Archives Board R-B 4780J

An almost dry marsh 20 miles east of Saskatoon, June 1959.

Surviving in next year country

"From the valley of the Red River-of-the-North to the foothills of the Rocky Mountains, we Canadian-Americans occupy one of world's great grassland regions, bounded by desert to the south and enclosed by various kinds of forest—coniferous and deciduous—on the west, north and east. North American grasslands mark the transitional zone between a predictably arid desert climate and a predictably moist forest climate. Desert climates grow small thorny shrubs, forest climates grow large trees, and, in between, a sward of grasses and herbs dominate, surviving wind and drought, fire and grazing, by hiding their perennial parts underground. They draw back in the face of adversity, tough out the bad times and break out with renewed vigour when the good times roll. Their community is diverse, multi-cultural, consisting of many different groups able to accommodate in different ways to the unstable fluctuating environment. They demonstrate what it takes to survive and blossom in the rain-shadow of the Rockies". – Stan Rowe, *Home Place*, 1990

Dealing with drought

The ability to endure the extremes of the northern prairie climate is one of the mysteries of the Red Lily. How does a plant that lacks the many obvious adaptations to a dry climate—finely dissected leaves, protective hairs or a rosette of ground hugging leaves—manage to survive under a regime of prolonged drought or in exposed hillside habitats with sandy soil? Part of the answer must be the storage of food and moisture in the bulb. The bulbous characteristic that enables the plant to survive unfavourable growing conditions, such as a winter, could also enable a plant to survive dry summer periods. "The mature lily is definitely a dry land plant, sometimes almost a desert plant, in its behaviour. It can withstand an extraordinary amount of drought when fully developed." [39] The Red Lily is notable among the North American lilies for growing under the poorest of conditions.[40] Part of the answer is also the ability of the plant to cease growth. This is the conserving approach to growth rather than the dash to set seed that typifies most annual plants.

"Evidently the dry years had a great deal to do with the scarcity of the Red Lily, and, this should be noted carefully, it has taken all this time for it to become re-established."

— Isabel Priestly,
Report in the
Western Naturalist
1946

Viewed from above, a small aborted bud is seen here as a white dot nested within the terminal whorl of leaves.

In order to flower and set seed, lilies require favourable moisture conditions. If the plants encounter dry conditions in spring most flower buds will terminate growth. This can occur at more than one size of bud. In some cases, the tiny aborted bud is similar in size to what it was before the shoot emerged; in other instances the bud has enlarged to several centimetres when it begins to yellow and die. Since only the bud stops growing, the entire stalk and green leaves continue to manufacture food for the bulb. At this point the lily looks like a stalked, vegetative plant with a terminal whorl of leaves. Under drought conditions, such as in the spring of 1998, we have seen most of the lilies within our research plots terminate flower development before the time of flowering. An average of 86% of the flowering plants in seven research plots terminated bud development. During a prolonged drought, from 2001 to 2003, the majority of stalked plants present in the plots were vegetative plants. Only under moist growing conditions such as in 1996 and in 1999 did this trend reverse.

A contrast of the number of plants with aborted buds and flowers in a dry year (1998) and a wet year (1999). Each flower symbol represents ten flowers (red) or aborted buds (white).

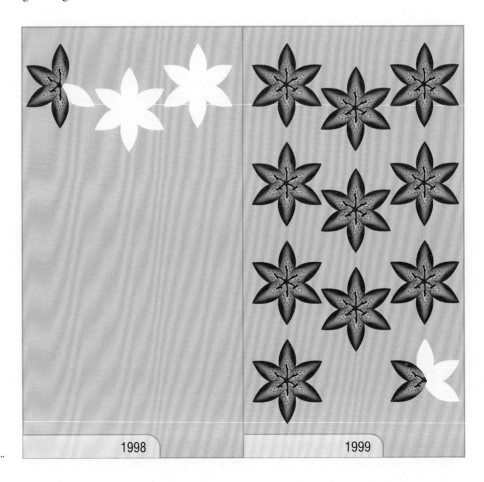

1998   1999

Waiting out the tough times

Seeds are not just a means of packaging genetic material to enhance spatial dispersal within the environment. They are also a means of extending the presence of the plant over time. Seeds are able to wait. When humans began cultivating plants for food it was important to have plants that would germinate reliably. Consequently we tend to think of seed dormancy (the failure of a mature, intact seed to germinate under favourable moisture, light, oxygen and temperature conditions) as a nuisance characteristic of some weedy species whose seeds maintain viability after years of sitting in the soil. Seed dormancy is a common and beneficial characteristic of many wild plants, whereas reliable germination is a trait selected for in domesticated plants.

There are many mechanisms for maintaining seed dormancy and *Lilium philadelphicum* seeds exhibit a combination of several types. In one, the seeds require exposure to a period of cold temperatures to ensure germination. This is an obvious mechanism to protect the seeds from germinating prior to the onset of winter. Another mechanism is to package chemical inhibitors within the seed coat that must be leached out by water to enable germination. This ensures that growing conditions must be moist before the embryo within the seed becomes active.

Seeds are shed from the pods throughout the year, even in winter as shown here, exposing them to various conditions unsuitable for growth.

Seeds of the Red Lily are extremely variable in their response to planting. A small proportion of lily seeds do not exhibit seed dormancy,[41] but most lily seeds require a period of chilling for germination (see Appendix V). Washing the seeds also increases germination, particularly if the seeds are collected in a dry year or from plants that produced several flowers per stalk. The variation in seed dormancy of the Red Lily is the plant equivalent of not carrying all your eggs in the same basket. Having seeds that can wait throughout a variety of climatic conditions helps lilies to survive the cyclical periods of prolonged drought that are part of a typical prairie climate.

PARTNERSHIP WITH FUNGI

It is curious that Red Lily bulbs have only a few shallow roots, whereas many plants faced with the unpredictable moisture on the prairies have extensive root systems. How do lilies manage?

Red Lilies rely on the extraordinary powers of fungi that live in the soil to enhance their ability to take up water and nutrients. This kind of partnership between a fungus and a vascular plant, such as the lily, is known as a mycorrhizal association (myco = fungus, rhiza = root). In these associations, the fungus, in exchange for carbohydrates such as starch, improves the vascular plant's ability to take up water, and delivers nutrients that are difficult for the plant to access, such as phosphate.[42] Thread-like fungal structures called 'hyphae' form a large network that vastly increases the absorptive area of the lily roots within the soil.

In the case of the Red Lily, the fungal hyphae actually enter the plant's root cells, where they produce visible sack-like vesicles and branching tree-like structures called arbuscules, as well as coils of hyphae. In our lily root samples, we found mostly hyphal coils. Plants collected in fall revealed some vesicles. Roots with side branches had the largest numbers of fungal structures. A number of specimens were covered with spores and external hyphae.

We suspect that mycorrhizal associations are ubiquitous in Red Lilies in natural populations. They were found in plants collected from Aspen Parkland habitats in Alberta[43] and we found them in plants collected at all of our study sites.

Arrows point to hyphal coils in the cells of a lily root seen greatly magnified by a microscope (X63).

The sleeping lily bulb

'Nature does not readily reveal her secrets' is a commonly expressed sentiment of field biologists and naturalists. The complexity, synchrony and interactions of the natural world become more apparent the more detailed the inquiry. Each discovery leads to more questions. We sense, as we investigate within the living world, that some things operate by trickster logic. Indeed there is more to life than meets the eye.

The sleeping lily bulb—a plant that skips a year or more of growth—is a puzzle to us. We have carefully tagged and measured plants in research plots (each about the size of two double beds) for up to ten years. Each plot is divided into one metre square quadrants and at least twice during each growing season, we search the ground for signs of lilies. We don't try to distinguish the grass-like cotyledons or even the tiny first true leaves (there is too much growing there), but we rarely miss the larger strap-shaped leaves or the stalked vegetative plants. Indeed, we have become experienced at finding chewed-off stalks or plants crisped by botrytis blight. Yet year after year we find new flowering lilies in our plots. From our knowledge of planting seedlings, this means that these 'new' flowering plants must have been present in the past as a stalked form. There are also a very small number (less than 2%) of previously tagged flowering plants that reappear as flowering plants after an absence of one, two and up to four years. In the most unusual case, a plant that grew as a flowering plant in 1996 was not seen again in any form until 2001, when it reappeared as a flowering plant.

In our plantings we have seen absenteeism of lilies after all stages of growth. Within a linear planting of ten individuals, of which five had flowered and five were stalked vegetative plants the previous year (1999), four out of ten were absent the following year (2000) and all four reappeared the subsequent year (2001). There are plenty of examples of absenteeism in the living world. That insects undergo diapause (a period of suspended development or growth, accompanied by greatly decreased metabolism) for more than one year is an unusual but known phenomenon. It is common to speak of dormancy in tulip bulbs and gladioli corms when we lift them from the garden and store them for an extended period of time, but lily bulbs which lack a tough outer skin will dry out more easily and are generally thought of by gardeners to be incapable of prolonged dormancy. Could the Red Lily maintain a 'non-growing state' in the soil, as long as the bulb neither rots nor dries out? Why not? Clearly there is no one-size-fits-all explanation, even within a single, simple patch of lilies.

> "Mrs. E. C. Boon of Tullis, Sask, reports that red lilies were quite prevalent last summer [1947], 'usually we just find the odd one; never more than three or four in one spot. It was a pleasant surprise to find them so numerous. In 1938 and 1939 there were none in the pasture which, last July, was dotted with them.' " [44]

Is there such a thing as too much moisture?

Cool damp conditions are ideal for the growth of various fungal diseases to which many native plants are susceptible. Botrytis blight (caused by *Botrytis cinerea* and *B. elliptica*) is a common disease of lilies whether wild or garden varieties. There are no known resistant plants. It is spread by tiny spores carried by wind currents or water splash. Germination of the spores occurs in damp, wet or humid conditions. The fungal hyphae, which grow at temperatures between 0° C and 26° C, develop as a greyish web on diseased tissue. The infection is first noted as a small white or brown spot on a leaf or bud and can spread throughout the stem and flower or developing pod, if favourable conditions exist. The likelihood of infection is increased if the

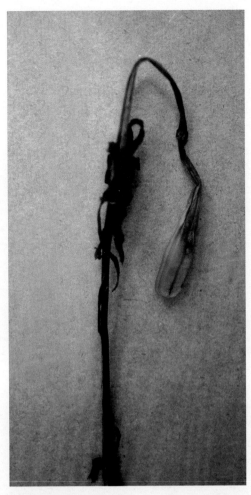
Botrytis blight on a lily stem bearing a pod.

plants have been damaged by hail, frost or other external forces, but healthy tissue is not immune. In addition, the fungus can live and grow on dead plant material, making it very persistent. Hot, dry weather prevents fungal growth and, hence, the disease.[45]

Dense stands of lilies growing in low areas where cool, moist air tends to pool are particularly vulnerable to a botrytis blight infection. Pod development and seed set can be severely affected. As described by Synge, "Too much wet weather and too low temperatures not only cause failure in the germination and growth of pollen, but encourage *Botrytis* infection of the seed capsules, which rapidly spreads to the seeds themselves…However slight the infection of the seed capsules the seeds they contain will not germinate." [46]

The vegetative plants are also susceptible to botrytis blight, turning brown or black and withering in mid-July, and thereby shortening the season for photosynthesis and storage of starch in the bulb. Badly affected lilies look scorched, becoming blackened and shrivelled as if burnt. 'Lily Fire' is a common name for *Botrytis elliptica*, a species of *Botrytis* particularly prevalent in lilies.[47] Ironically, a real fire would benefit such a stand. In a horticultural setting removal and burning of garden debris and infected stalks is important in controlling botrytis blight.

Late frost and its effect on flowering

The first lily plants to emerge in the spring are those with small bulbs, closest to the soil surface. Plants bearing flower buds are the last, rarely emerging before the last week of May. They are first visible as a shoot with the already-formed bud tightly clothed in protective leaves. It takes another two to three weeks for the stem to elongate and the leaves to open, until finally the terminal whorl of leaves reveals the green flower bud.

If there is a late June frost, as occurred in 2004, the exposed buds will suffer frost damage and wither, but late maturing flower shoots, with leaves still protecting the buds, will continue to develop. It is the buds that are primarily affected, not the leafy parts. Frost can have two effects: first, it reduces the total number of flowers and second, it can skew the 'observed' flowering period. Since only late developing flowers mature, the blooming period appears delayed.

Two vegetative plants "scorched" by
botrytis blight.

CHAPTER 5

"[Wild fires] presented a terrifying sight to the settlers, especially at night, resembling a necklace as they swept over the distant hills. The prairie, thus cleansed of its dead grass the fall before, now resembled a vast green lawn, dotted with purple crocuses, later with clusters of blue violets. As the summer advanced the everchanging panorama of colour delighted the eyes of the younger pioneers. ... In our many joyous ramblings we came upon many species of wild flowers that are seldom seen today, such as fringed and bottled gentian, dusty pink primroses and shooting star and spicy seneca-root—much sought by the Indians. But outstanding in our memory were the flaming patches of red lilies, encircling the alkaline marshlands in hundreds." – Mrs. T. H. Bray and Mrs. Hilda Newton, *Nature 1904-1955*, 1955

Fire and the phoenix

Fire is a natural event in grassland habitats in Saskatchewan. In a dry climate such as ours, dead vegetation decays slowly, building up on the surface annually to form a continuous blanket of fuel. Enough fuel can accumulate for fires to occur every few years; the interval depends on the vegetation community and growing conditions. All that is required is a source of ignition, and both natural (lightning) and human sources are available.

Grass fires remove the surface vegetation (called thatch) but because they move quickly across the ground, they have little effect below the surface. In experimental spring fires in grassland communities near Saskatoon, the soil temperature changed very little at 5 cm down, even though the temperature on the surface reached over 200°C and, at 10 cm above the ground, over 400°C.[48] Even at 1 cm deep, there was no increase in temperature in spring and fall burns in fescue grassland near Saskatoon. The soil temperature did rise to 44°C in midsummer burns as a result of greater accumulation of fuels and drier soils. This temperature, however, is still well below the 60°C considered fatal to plant tissues.[49]

Large Red Lily bulbs typically sit between 3 and 5 cm below the surface, with their roots emerging from the bottom of the bulb at 5 cm deep or slightly deeper. At this level, depending on site factors such as level of thatch build-up and soil characteristics, they are untouched by most fires.

Rather than harming lilies, fire seems to rejuvenate them and may stimulate a mass flowering as observed by Frank Pfeiffer after a fall fire on his land northeast of Saskatoon.

"After the fire, the number of lilies was unbelievable—I have seen nothing like it before or since. Lilies in small numbers had been seen there for years: the land, about 20 acres, was not suitable for crops as it was sour and stony with an alkali slough. The higher land was hayed late in the season for the prairie wool. There were thousands of lilies growing in the pasture the year after the fire in early fall." – Frank Pfeiffer, survey participant, Saskatoon, 2004

Lily plant with three stalks, all with pods, shows the depth of the bulb in the soil. The deepest bulb is about 8 cm to the base of the bulb. The two bulbs above it are just over 5 cm to their bases. This plant, which was dug in fall after a spring fire, shows the large number of pods that can be produced in a post-fire growing season.

New growth on blackened soil two weeks after a prairie fire in late May. Emerging lily plants are clearly visible in the absence of other vegetation. Left to right:
1. Tips of grass leaves were singed during the fire.
2. Strap-shaped lily leaf
3. Vegetative plant
4. Flower shoot just emerging from the ground.

The sudden appearance of vivid red lily flowers after a fire inspired the name 'prairie phoenix.' The phoenix was a mythical bird "said to burn itself to ashes on a funeral pyre, and rise again from the ashes, fresh and beautiful, for another long life."[50] The term 'phoenix' plant has been used to refer to annuals that germinate or become established only on sites that have been burned.[51] Candace Savage also refers to the response of grasses to fire as phoenix-like.[52] Our use broadens the term to include our perennial lily, whose magnificent flowering is greatly enhanced by fires.

Avoiding the heat

Part of the lily's strategy for coping with fire is avoidance. Not only are the bulbs situated at a depth that avoids heating, but the above-ground growth stages are of relatively short duration. Flowering shoots remain underground until early June, in general. When the shoots do emerge, they elongate quickly and flower in about a month. By late summer, most growth activity has ceased and the nutrients have been safely stored in the bulb. For the eight months from October to May, the only part of the lily plant above ground is the dry seed stalk.

Another way that lilies cope with fire is to wait underground for years like a coiled spring until released by a trigger such as fire. Having shoots ready and waiting to grow, means that at a moment's notice, the plants can begin to send a flower stalk into full sunlight with little competition for space from neighbouring plants. In addition, fire, while releasing lilies for growth, has other effects on their environment. It has been noted, for instance, that light and warm temperatures can stimulate mycorrhizal fungi to produce spores and colonize roots.[53] Red lilies, with their massive stores of starch in bulb scales, and shoots ready to elongate in early June, would stand to benefit from the stimulating effects that thatch removal might have on fungi with which they have a mycorrhizal association.

Flame red lilies contrast with vibrant green
vegetation seven weeks after a spring fire
cleansed the site.

PRAIRIE FIRE, CLOSE UP

In a wave of intense colour, brilliant heat and a hissing-whistling sound, the fire edge moves irregularly, darting, then slowing, licking the edges of the pocket gopher mounds, revealing the tiny topography of anthills and tufts of little bluestem. It moves quickly, leaving charred and bent grass stalks to topple into a horizontal mat of grey ash. Over all, the pallor of smoke lingers briefly. Shrubs, seared and left standing, will grow anew from the roots. The mobile insects, birds and mammals have taken flight; others have found refuge in underground abodes.

Rising from the ashes

We documented a rejuvenation of lilies at Last Mountain Lake National Wildlife Area, where controlled burning is used as a tool in habitat management. Before fire passed through, we noted only two flowering lilies. Both were robust plants with two flowers growing in tall grass in our 3 m by 4 m research plot as shown in the top line of the diagram opposite. The fire swept through the area the next spring about two weeks before the lilies emerged from the ground. Six weeks later, eight plants were blooming in addition to the two seen the previous year. Six of these plants had single flowers, but there were three plants with two flowers and one with three flowers. Each flower produced a mature pod (15 pods in total). Estimating a modest average of 200 seeds per pod, the total seed production in this 3 m by 4 m research plot would have been 3,000 seeds!

In the year following the fire, 1997, the number of flowering plants in this research plot more than doubled and the number of plants with more than one flower per head jumped from four to twelve: six plants had two flowers, five had three flowers and one had four. All these flowers produced pods but none was left standing at the end of the season; all had been chewed off at a height of 3 to 10 cm above ground and removed by the last week in September. The culprit may have been a deer mouse, a seed-eater and one of the first small mammals to come into an area after a fire.[54]

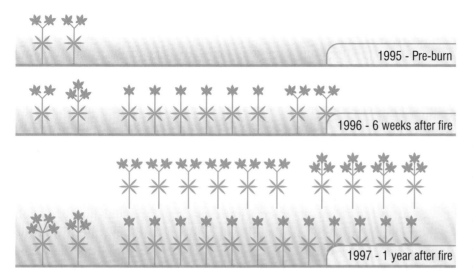

1995 - Pre-burn

1996 - 6 weeks after fire

1997 - 1 year after fire

Profile of lily flowering the year before (1995) and the two seasons after (1996 and 1997) a spring prairie fire. Two plants had flowers the year before the fire passed through. Six weeks after a late May fire, 8 additional plants bloomed, several with multiple flowers. A year later, the number of flowering plants more than doubled (going from 10 to 24) and the number of plants with more than one flower went from four to twelve.

1 week

3 weeks

7 weeks

14 weeks

Regrowth following a prairie fire in late May: blackened soil one week after the fire; spring growth at three weeks; midsummer vegetation, with lily flowers, at seven weeks; seed heads at 14 weeks.

Spring fire or fall fire?

The extent of the flowering response after a fire depends on timing. If a fire occurs before the middle of September, it may stimulate plants that are still in the later stages of shoot development to set flowers for the following season. A fire in August or early September could cause every lily with sufficient bulb reserves to set out a flower shoot for the following spring, producing the "thousands of lilies" that Frank Pfeiffer describes in his quotation above.

A spring fire, on the other hand, occurs too late to cause an increase in the number of plants that set flowers, as this is an activity done in the fall. A fire that occurs before the plants emerge, however, can rejuvenate a lily population by stimulating growth in the flower shoots that have been waiting underground for years. In the case of a spring fire, the major flowering response to fire is seen in the year after the fire, when the number of plants that flower goes up and the number of flowers per plant also increases. This two-year response after a spring fire is illustrated in the diagram on the previous page, based on observations made in one of our research plots at Last Mountain Lake.

How long between fires?

Short-term benefits in the first and second year after burning are readily observed, but how long do the benefits last? Our estimate is about five years. In our 3 m by 4 m research plot at Last Mountain Lake, flower numbers remained relatively steady (with good seed set) for five years after the fire, while the total number of plants in the population doubled. In the sixth year, the number of flowering plants fell to two, then to zero with no seed set in years 7, 8 and 9 after the fire. Insects devoured many of the flowers in the sixth year after the fire. In year 8, when small mammals were especially numerous, many of the bulbs were dug out of the ground. In the ninth year after the fire, 67% of the plants in the population had no above-ground growth at all, including the two plants first noted at the site in 1995.

Pods on lily plants growing at a site burned four years previously. The plant on the left has four pods, the one on the right, three.

Lilies, when numerous, had become targets for insects and mammals (small and large) and, in the absence of fires, thatch build-up provided protective habitat for these herbivores. At this particular site, the lilies would have benefited from a second fire four or five years after the first to remove further thatch accumulation. In the absence of a fire, some bulbs will undoubtedly build up their reserves again through photosynthesis by single leaves and vegetative stalks, eventually becoming large enough to form flowering shoots to sit and wait for the next signal to flower. Meanwhile, throughout the area, the tens of thousands of seeds produced in the first five post-fire years will be establishing plants with diverse genetic material if they can find moist bare ground for germination and establishment.

Philip Taylor CWS

WHAT DO MICE AND VOLES DO IN A PRAIRIE FIRE?

"Striking, but indirect, evidence of small mammals fleeing fire comes from watching raptors during controlled burns at Last Mountain Lake National Wildlife Area. Swainson's Hawks, and to a lesser extent, Northern Harriers, arrive quickly at fires in progress and hover over the fire front, often in the smoke, at heights varying usually from 5 - 10 m or so above ground. They can be seen dropping to the ground, in both the burned and unburned grassland, presumably in pursuit of mice and voles. I have occasionally seen them carry off a small unidentified rodent, so it is obviously well worth their while. Of all the raptor species present in the area when we burn—three owls, one harrier, three buteos, two falcons, one accipiter—the Swainson's Hawk is by far the quickest to respond, the most commonly seen, and the one that remains for the longest period of time, from near the start of the fire until well after the smoke has ceased. Swainson's Hawks have arrived from several kilometres away, and as many as eight birds have attended one fire—more than one family group! I would call this hawk a truly fire-adapted species because of this foraging technique. The harrier is more of an opportunist; it does not seem to stay around for long periods of time or assemble in large numbers (one or two maximum) when a fire is burning." – Philip Taylor, Habitat Biologist, Canadian Wildlife Service, 2004

The drama of lily populations

Looking at the lily patch

Our study began with questions about the dynamics of lily populations. Why do lilies bloom one year and then 'disappear?' What makes a good lily year? Do lilies still bloom abundantly?

In order to answer these questions we tagged flowering lilies within a discrete area, a research plot of 3 m by 4 m, and monitored them in late spring, early summer and early fall. It soon became apparent that in addition to flowering plants there were two forms of non-flowering plants: the strap-shaped leaves and the leafy stalks that we call vegetative plants. Not all of these were necessarily younger than flowering plants. There were also discrete groupings of plants that were so tightly positioned they could have come from a single origin. For lack of a better term we refer to them as a 'clan.' Each year as new plants appeared in our research plots, they were measured, mapped and described. Over the years we have also added research plots, particularly at Last Mountain Lake National Wildlife Area, in order to study lily populations under management practices of controlled burning and pulse grazing (intense grazing for short periods).

Studying the same small patches of ground for ten years gives one perspective. We have watched as some of our tagged plants have meandered slowly through the soil, while others have shown a fidelity to the original tag position. By sideways growth, the bulb can displace itself by a centimetre a year but the emerging shoots are also capable of growing laterally several centimetres from the bulb before emerging from the soil. A mat of pussytoes can speed the change in position of a lily plant; a new anthill or gopher mound can provide some elbow room. Stop-action cameras help us to understand the rapid movement of a hummingbird. Time lapse photography, used over a span of years, is needed to follow many perennial plants that move like slow clouds constantly changing shape and position. To be fully appreciated, the slow dance of the lilies, with entrances, exits and costume changes, needs a patient audience.

Costume changes

Once a lily plant has developed to the stage where the bulb can initiate a flowering shoot, one would expect that, as long as conditions permit, a flowering shoot would grow each year. In fact, repeated flowering is only one of several possibilities and not the only outcome. In our ten-year study, some plants flowered consistently for six years in a row, whereas others loosely alternated between producing a flowering stalk one year, a vegetative stalk the next year to return as a flowering stalk and so on. In the year following flowering, a plant may grow as a vegetative plant with a leafy stalk, it may show no above-ground growth or it may produce two stalks where there was one. These are the basic costume changes we have observed. In addition, early in the growing season, a flowering shoot may terminate growth of the flower bud (becoming an aborted bud plant) and thus dramatically change its appearance by essentially changing its hat.

One of our original questions was 'what makes lily populations appear one year and disappear the next?' To answer this, we looked at the fate of individual plants in the year after they flowered—did they flower again or did they grow in some other less visible form? We have combined the information on 510 observations of plants that flowered within a seven-year period (1995 to 2002) in the pie chart 'Seven Year Average.' The largest portion of the 'pie' or about one-third of the plants flowered again in the second year. For the remaining two-thirds, flowering was not followed by another year of flowering. What happened in their second year varied: about one-fifth had their stalks chewed off by insects or mammals before midsummer; one-sixth grew as vegetative plants and another sixth had no above-ground growth; one-tenth were plants with aborted buds; and a small portion produced several stems close together (a clan) or only strap-shaped leaves.

This is the long-term average, composed of information from a series of years. The accompanying figures are profiles of four of these years. These illustrate that the size of the pie pieces shift from year to year as individual plants change form in response to changing circumstances. Weather, as well as growing conditions when the plant forms next year's shoot and the number of herbivores present, will affect what we see when we look at a population of lilies.

In 1997, the populations were dramatically affected by vole activity. The largest portion, as shown in the figure, represents plants that were chewed off in the year after flowering; the second largest group is plants with no sign of above-ground growth. In 1998, the early growing season was hot and dry. In this year, the largest portion of the plants that had flowered the previous year grew as plants with aborted buds. In 2000, moist conditions, which began in 1999, resulted in almost three-quarters of the plants flowering for two years in

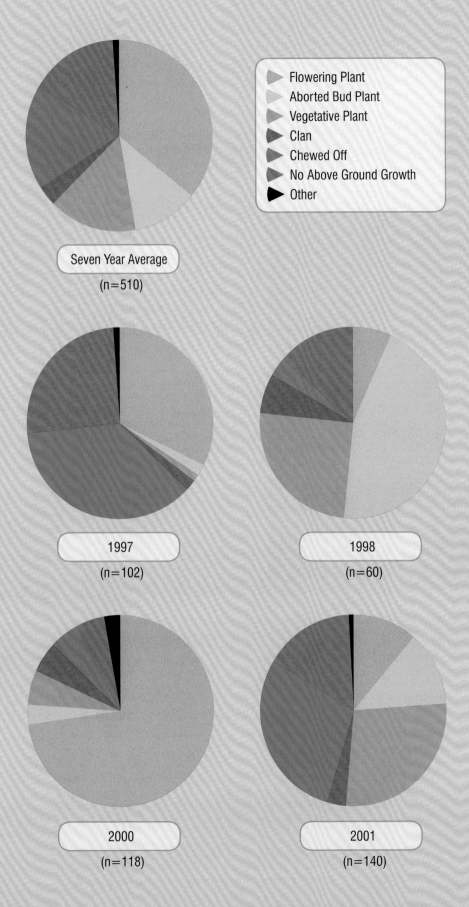

Seven Year Average

(n=510)

1997

(n=102)

1998

(n=60)

2000

(n=118)

2001

(n=140)

Legend:
- Flowering Plant
- Aborted Bud Plant
- Vegetative Plant
- Clan
- Chewed Off
- No Above Ground Growth
- Other

Seven year average

This seven year average is based on 510 observations of plants that flowered between 1995 and 2002 and shows what they did the year after flowering. Some plants (184) flowered two years in a row, but many did not. Small mammals and insects chewed off the stalks or flowers of 90 of them, 57 plants had aborted buds, 78 reverted to a vegetative form after flowering, 78 produced no above-ground growth at all, 18 grew as clans and 5 reappeared as strap-shaped leafs.

1997

In 1997, lily populations were dramatically affected by vole activity. Of the 102 plants that flowered in 1996, we observed in 1997 that 36% had chewed-off stalks, 33% flowered again, 25% had no above-ground growth (this number includes an undetermined number of plants that had their stalk chewed to the ground in early spring), 2% were plants with aborted buds, 2% grew as clans, 1% were vegetative plants.

1998

In 1998, drought conditions during the growing season resulted in a large number of plants with aborted buds. Of the 60 plants that flowered in 1997, we observed in 1998 that 45% were plants with aborted buds, 25 % were vegetative plants, 13% had no above-ground growth, 7% flowered again, 7% grew as clans and 3% had chewed-off stalks.

2000

In 2000, the moist conditions, begun in 1999, continued resulting in a high number of flowers. Of the 118 plants that flowered in 1999, we observed in 2000 that 73% flowered again, 6% were vegetative plants, 5% grew as clans, 5% had no above-ground growth, 5% had chewed-off stalks, 3% were plants with aborted buds and 3% were strap-shaped leaves.

2001

In 2001, many mature plants grew as vegetative plants due to dry weather in late summer and fall of the previous year. High small mammal and insect populations were also prevalent. Of the 140 plants that flowered in 2000, we observed in 2001 that 29% had chewed-off stalks, 28% were vegetative plants, 16% had no above-ground growth, 13% were plants with aborted buds, 11% flowered again and 4% grew as clans.

a row. In 2001, many plants that had flowered in 2000 grew as vegetative plants as a result of dry conditions in the previous late summer and fall. High mammal and insect numbers in 2001 resulted in an equal number of plants with stalks chewed off by midsummer.

It is important to note that not all plants respond to growing conditions in the same way, although most do. Behind these numbers there is an underlying variability in the growth pattern of individual plants.

The size of the chorus

The vagaries of a lily's life due to weather, herbivores, competition from other plants and perturbations to the immediate habitat, mean that every area with a few flowering lilies will often contain many other unseen lily plants. During ten years of monitoring lily populations, we have observed that the number of plants that flower in a research plot can range from 2% to 61% depending on the year, while the total number of plants in these plots stayed pretty much the same. When lily flowers disappear, it does not necessarily mean that the plants are dead; many change to camouflage attire and become hard to see.

Another costume change. A two-flowered lily with an old stalk with four pods. Some plants exhibit changes in the number of flowers in a head, rising and falling in many different sequences with changing growth conditions.

It is difficult to gauge the potential for flowering within any given population of lilies. From the surface one cannot know the density of the lily bulbs underground. If we assume that we have tagged the vast majority of lily plants within our research plots over the ten-year observation period, then we have a measure of the density of lily plants at that site. Our plot with the lowest density has two lilies per square metre or 24 per plot. Our plot with the greatest density has 15 per square metre or 183 per plot. The average density of the lilies within the plots begun in 1995 is ten plants per square metre, a far greater number than one would ever suspect from a casual look.

A STORY OF YELLOWS AND REDS

Consistent observation of a lily patch can reveal surprising information, as Doris Silcox discovered in a patch near Carlyle. Entries from an eleven-year diary follow.[55]

1978 - one yellow lily in patch of red-flowered lilies.

1979 - three yellow lily plants in patch of red-flowered lilies.

1980 - six yellow lily plants in patch with 129 red-flowered lilies. (One yellow lily plant on a steep clay bank which 'washed out,' exposing the bulb, was transplanted to yard.)

1981 - five yellow lily plants among many red-flowered lilies.

1982 - many lilies initially appeared but the entire patch was cleaned out by the picking of thoughtless travellers.

1983 - fewer lilies appeared and again they were all picked by travellers.

1984 - only one deformed red-flowered lily and no yellow lilies occurred at the roadside ditch site.

Brian Irving

1985 - no lilies appeared at the natural roadside ditch site although the three transplanted yellow lilies in the yard developed normally and bloomed.

1986 - again no lilies appeared at the roadside site, although the three transplanted lilies developed normally and would have bloomed, but on 2 June a hailstorm devastated them.

1987 - the lily patch at the roadside site made a remarkable recovery with 43 red-flowered lilies and 3 yellow lilies. One of the yellow lilies was collected as a voucher specimen for filing in the W. P. Fraser Herbarium, University of Saskatchewan, to document the distributional record.

1988 - no lilies bloomed at the natural ditch site, presumably because of extreme drought conditions; the three transplanted yellow lilies in the yard bloomed well, with one plant bearing three flowers.

What makes a good lily year?

Moisture is the key. It must be present in late spring and in the preceding growing season when the bulb is producing next year's plant. If moisture is present, along with other favourable conditions, such as warm spring weather and a disturbance that removes old vegetation from the surface, then these harmonious events can lead to a good show of flowers.

"Reports from various parts of the province show that the Red Lily is much more prevalent than usual. Perhaps if favourable seasons continue, we will have them back again in profusion. Mr. Cliff Shaw writes that in the Yorkton area there are a dozen this year for every one that bloomed last year. Hundreds of them bloomed in a meadow not over ten miles from Regina. The same is true in other meadows at various parts, where they have not been seen in large numbers for some time." – Lloyd Carmichael, *Botany*, 1947

"The Red Lily, Saskatchewan's Floral Emblem, staged a brave comeback this season [1945]. From widely separated points in the province came reports of 'hundreds blooming where in recent years there had been but an odd stray blossom.' "

Disturbance is a normal event in a healthy prairie ecosystem and is vital to many native plants. The positive response of the Red Lily to a wide array of disturbances from fire to grazing to digging by mammals, speaks to this plant's adaptations for renewal.

Fire is a tonic to lilies. It is important in providing a place in the sun and encouraging full growth, food production and subsequent bulb growth. Lilies may be adept at endurance, but they are not aggressive competitors. They are frequently confined to marginal environments where soils are too alkaline to allow full growth of other plants. In order to thrive they need the opportunity to maximize sunlight, growing space and nutrients. Fire brings about these conditions and results in a quick positive response.

Fire also plays a cleansing role by reducing sources of diseases like botrytis blight. The removal of thatch facilitates an important reprieve from small mammal populations that harvest the above-ground parts and the bulbs, especially evident in years of peak vole populations. The year 1997 could be described as a 'vole high' in many areas of the province, with meadow voles invading even the urban landscape. Our study areas were already experiencing small mammal chewing in 1996, with the majority of stalks chewed by the fall of that year. Most of the plants checked in the spring of 1997 were chewed, some right to the ground. By July, there was either nothing to be seen or chewed stalks at three-quarters of the tag positions in all three of our study sites. Only the research plots that had been burned in 1996 escaped the ravages of these rodents. Here, evidence of chewing wasn't seen until late in 1997. The burned plots had an abundance of flowers and only a few (5%) tag positions had no above-ground growth—the opposite of what happened elsewhere in 1997.

Fires are now unusual events. It has been noted that lilies are often more abundant on railway rights-of-way than in ditches along public highways. The thinking in the 1940s was that this reflected greater picking by travellers along roadsides.[56] A more likely reason was the common practice of burning along railroad tracks as a means of controlling unwanted plant growth. With each successive decade, burning slough margins and ditches adjacent to grid roads has become less common as a vegetation control practice, but local fires do escape, now and again, particularly under dry conditions.

Contrast of a wet year and a dry year at an alkali slough east of Saskatoon.

Grazing and haying activities help keep dominant plants in check. Flowering lilies can persist for years in pastures grazed annually by cattle. Survey participants reported flowering lilies in 2000 scattered over large areas of pasture grazed annually for 45 and 60 years. The pasture grazed for 60 years has produced lilies for at least the last 50.

"Grazing is a selective disturbance force which affects grassland vegetation in three ways: defoliation, trampling, and nutrient cycling. Light to moderate grazing controls build-up of organic matter. Trampling helps break down plant material and exposes soil to serve as a seed bed. Consumed plant matter is returned to the system as waste for soil nutrient cycling." – Garry Trottier, *Conservation of Canadian Prairie Grasslands*, 1992

The extent to which lilies increase or decrease under grazing pressure presumably depends on a number of factors, such as the habitat type, the number of grazers and soil texture. Hooves can compact firm ground and, in soft soil such as along wetland margins, they punch holes, disrupting lily bulbs, some of which get pushed too deep to grow.

Grazing practices that mimic historic patterns of bison grazing can produce good conditions for lily flowering. We had a chance to observe this on a relatively dry upland at the north end of Last Mountain Lake. One of our research plots was exposed to large numbers of cattle that grazed native grassland for a limited period in a deferred rotation, a grazing practice called 'pulse grazing.' The plot was within an area frequented by 82 head of cattle for one year from early June to late September: hooves pounded the ground, while mouths trimmed the growing vegetation, and urine and piles of manure fertilized the ground. An adjacent research plot was not grazed or trampled as it was fenced to keep cattle out.

In the grazed plot, the number of flowering plants increased by one-third in the first year after grazing and doubled in the second year. In the plot from which cattle were excluded, there was no increase in the number of flowering plants the following year or in the year after. What's more, the number of flowers per stem increased dramatically in the grazed plot in the second year after the cattle were present. One plant went from three flowers to six—the only plant with six flowers that we saw in ten years of research in the area.

The combination of a good rain following the removal of thatch by grazing resulted in a good show of lilies according to Evelyn Boon of Tullis: "After a wet year in '51 and an early spring, we too, were blessed with more than usual wild flowers....It was the Western Red Lilies—our beloved Tiger Lilies—that surprised us most. My brother-in-law's pasture has a small coulee running through it. As far as we could see, the lilies dotted the bottom of the coulee. On the grazed portion they were so big and dark colored. We even found them in the ditch along the road this spring. Two or three flowers on one stalk were common. Some had four on them." [57]

Lily populations also tolerate haying, even when it is done annually for many years. Owners of a pasture near Aberdeen told us in 2000 that their pasture, which has been cut in August annually since 1902, still turns orange with lilies in years with enough rain.

Soil disturbance events such as pocket gopher activity or roadwork that provide breaks in a thick vegetative cover can create a localized abundance of blooms if moisture conditions are right. One anecdotal observation was of a farmer unintentionally pulling harrows into a corner patch of native prairie with the result that many lilies flowered the following year where few had been

A profusion of flowering lilies is eye-catching from a distance. Stems bearing four, five and six flowers are stunning up close.

....

Jim Sullivan

George Tosh

observed before. Similarly, where a ditch had been sliced open to insert a gas pipeline, a procession of lilies grew along the cutline like flagging stakes.

The importance of disturbance events often comes as a surprise to the observer, such as survey participant Virginia Perron of Spalding: "I have been interested in wild flowers since my childhood, and the Red Lily (Tiger Lily, Prairie Lily) has been my highlight. It is elusive, as I remember years that they have hardly shown up and years (this year) that they are plentiful. On July 2nd, Velma Spizawka and I went to our old haunt, across the tracks, close to town and we found them quite plentiful. The mystery is that, over the years, in order to maintain the railroad track, they would bulldoze a wide strip on either side and clear it of brush and vegetation, and I can't understand how, in two or three years all the wild flowers and vegetation were back in all their glory. So it was with the lilies. In an area that had originally been bulldozed, we found a large patch of lilies, some in bloom, many in bud. Besides the lilies, we found a lot of lady-slippers that I hadn't seen in that area before!"

PLACES OF RENEWAL

"It may seem paradoxical that disturbances of the prairie by digging animals, floods, fire and even local overgrazing were essential to maintenance of the fully developed prairie itself. Close examination of luxuriant grassland will usually show that here and there all the plants that become conspicuous during succession actually persist on the prairie at all times. They are able to sustain themselves in suitable microhabitats made by gopher mounds, badger diggings, anthills, drifted soil and abandoned mouse runways....When we see harvester ants, ground squirrels and other disturbers of the soil, we should thank them for cultivating spots where lesser plants can persist in readiness to renew the land in time of need." – David Costello, *The Prairie World*, 1969

A multitude of flaming lilies

Donna Stang

"There were probably lilies covering the whole quarter section and adjacent ones that year [1997]" – Donna Stang, survey participant, Avonlea, 2000

We greatly admire large numbers of densely blooming lilies, the 'red patches of prairie.' Such abundant floral displays gladden the heart. These flamboyant expressions of beauty are one of the unique gifts that Saskatchewan residents want to pass on to future generations. "To the children of Saskatchewan in the hope that every child may know the joy of seeing the spirit of midsummer embodied in a multitude of flaming lilies" is the dedication of Dorothy Morrison's book *The Prairie Lily*.

This chorus of colour we so much admire is also good for the lilies. Large patches of red undoubtedly attract the attention of pollinators and, with many plants in flower, there are increased opportunities for out-crossing and good seed set. It seems likely that lilies rely on these years to produce quantities of viable seed.

After a mass blooming event, the lily flower numbers may drop alarmingly, making people think that the population has disappeared altogether. In the past, such disappearances have been attributed to picking by 'thoughtless passers-by,' but there are other causes for the absence of flowers. When flowering lilies grow in large, dense masses, they become targets for herbivores, such as voles, deer and certain insects. In our studies, the number of stems chewed by small mammals increased dramatically following good lily years (1996 and 1999-2000). A contributing factor is that small mammals, such as the meadow vole, also increase in response to the lush growth and plentiful food supply available in good lily years.

Those of us familiar with the prairies know that a cycle of moist years is all too quickly followed by drought. In dry years, a show of Red Lilies is rare. Under dry conditions, the plants don't necessarily die; they wait, conserving their resources to bloom again.

The longevity of lilies

Once a lily bulb is large enough to produce a vegetative or flowering stalk, it usually produces only a single stalk year after year. We also know that the stalk itself lasts but a summer and that the roots and bulb scales last a little over two years before being replaced. The constant flow of stored food and replenishment of food reserves can theoretically maintain a plant for an indefinite number of years unless it is entirely eaten, ploughed up, starved by competitive plants or severe drought, or any combination of adverse events.

Plant with three stems growing from one bulb.

Instances also occur when suddenly there are two stalks where there had been one. Approximately 4% of the 510 flowering plants with single stems shown in the pie chart 'Seven Year Average' have in subsequent years formed clans (tight groupings of stalked plants), particularly under good growing conditions. The two plots that exhibited this growth response most frequently (12 out of 18 instances) were in areas that had experienced burning, grazing and good moisture, the closest approximation to classic pre-settlement conditions.

"There are Lilies, Blue Bells, wild rose trees, native grass and what I have called Buck-brush and Wolf Willow. The lilies have been there as long as I can remember. I am 81 years old."

The bulb of the robust plant on page 30 showing the position of detached scales that are growing bulblets.

Another way in which a clan may occur is when some of the outer scales become separated from the mature parent bulb. In one case, 12 new bulbs were found in the vicinity of the oldest portion of a bulb cluster. Each one of these new bulbs could produce a stalked plant in the future.

The mythical phoenix was said to live 500 years and then be reborn from its ashes to youthful vigour. Our 'prairie phoenix' is capable of a very long life and of responding to natural disturbance with renewal of growth. Although it is impossible to age a lily as one can a tree, the stories of our elders attest to the longevity that is possible in a patch of lilies.

Lessons from the lily patch

When we look at individual lily flowers, we notice subtly different hues, shapes of petals, and even size, colour and distribution of the spots. These are the outward expressions of genetic variability. Hidden from view are other traits that are similarly variable, such as differences in growth patterns: the plants that flower year after year, those that rarely initiate flowers, the seasonally early bloomers and the late, the slow growers and the ones that progress steadily to flower. Wild lily populations are amazingly diverse in form and response. Variety is more than the spice of life; it is the essence.

No two years in the lily patch are ever the same. Each year brings some 'new' aspect to our attention. This can be a

Field of lilies near Conquest

Roy Whitely

different insect that eats the plant, an unusual climatic condition such as a late June frost, or the digging and harvesting by a small mammal. Each of these events has an impact on the lily plants. What has been equally fascinating is the large array of other plants and animals that interact in their own unique ways with the lily plants. We began by studying a single plant species and have been introduced to a varied assemblage, some of the threads in the web of a prairie world. Like threads in a tapestry, whose colours seem to change as they become interwoven, so the lily populations are affected by interactions with the other plants and animals.

Even after ten years, our study continues to be fascinating because it is about so much more than a single species of plant. It has enlarged and enriched our view of the world we share. It has been a rare opportunity to become intimately familiar with each patch of lilies. No two are the same. We have watched the thorny buffaloberry encroach in one research plot; in another, the arrival of a poplar sapling that, should it survive, will have a large impact in the next ten years. We have noted the presence of each new rose bush, often with heated comment. There have been many surprises, such as the persistent buzzing that alerted us to the bumble bee nest built within an abandoned vole nest;[58] the pile of vole droppings when one plot was the winter place of a communal toilet. Other aspects have become the expected. At one wetland site we listen for the now familiar tap-tapping of the Yellow Rail, at another the chug-a-lug of a bittern. A Red-tailed Hawk announces our arrival near its nest at an alkali slough. The hours spent on hands and knees, searching and measuring, are more than rewarded by the richness of life found there, the slow changes and the new surprises.

Bonnie recording observations on lilies in our research plot near Pike Lake.

Part 3
LILIES IN THE CHANGING LANDSCAPE

CHAPTER 7

Harebell

Hedysarum

Smooth camas

Ascending purple milk-vetch

Dean Nernberg, CWS

A vast open prairie

The carpeted plain

From the back of a horse somewhere between Last Mountain Lake and the Elbow Sand Hills, the Earl of Southesk remarked that "flowers of the gayest colour enlivened the landscape. The most common were the small tiger-lilies and the roses, and next came blue-bells and white strawberry blossoms. Sometimes acres and acres were covered with intermingled masses of the orange lily and the pendulous blue-bell, the whole of them so short of stem that the glory of the flowers combined with the rich greenness of their leaves, and it seemed as if a vast oriental carpet had been thrown upon the plain."[59]

A carpet of wild flowers

The date was July 7, 1859. Twenty years later, almost to the day, John Macoun was so impressed with the wild flowers near the north end of Last Mountain Lake that he named the area 'The Flower Garden of the North West.' In his notebook he wrote, "Flowers are a most conspicuous feature of the prairie. Hedysarum and various Astragali vying with the lily and vetch in loveliness and luxuriance. Often, whole acres would be red and purple with beautiful flowers and the air laden with the perfume of roses. Sometimes, lilies (Lilium philadelphicum) are so abundant that they cover an acre of ground, bright red. At others, they are mixed with other liliaceous plants, such as Zygadenus glaucus [Smooth Camas], and form a ring around thickets which we passed."[60]

Why were flowers so prolific in the mid-to-late 1800s? What were the prairies like? According to accounts written at the time, they were alternately rain-soaked and dry, trampled and soiled by herds of bison, chewed by grasshoppers and burned regularly in vast prairie fires.

Rain on the plain

Although dry years and drought occurred frequently, as in the early 1870s, and from 1884 to 1894,[61] travellers across Saskatchewan in 1857-58 and 1879-81 got drenched with rain. This included John Macoun, the Earl of Southesk and John Palliser.

Macoun kept daily notes on the weather during his travels across Saskatchewan in 1879, the year he discovered the 'flower garden' north of Last Mountain Lake. Rain fell on 21 days from June 19 to August 31—on average every third day. Heavy rain fell on June 19 and 24, July 2, 5, 23 and 24, and August 4.[62] In 1879, his assistant nearly drowned trying to cross the north end of Last Mountain Lake on a road he had used in a previous year.[63] Macoun also kept daily records in 1880 as he crossed the province on a more southern route. This year was even wetter than 1879, with rain on 31 dates within this period (on average, every other day), with heavy rain on June 21, 28 and 29, July 2, 3, 11 and 14, August 4, 10, 11, 14, 21, 22, 23 and 31. Not surprisingly, Macoun described the summers as warm "with an abundance of rain, but not necessarily a cloudy atmosphere."[64]

The Earl of Southesk also noted heavy rain on July 4, 6 and 7 between Qu'Appelle and the Elbow of the South Saskatchewan River 20 years earlier.[65] Palliser, heading west from Fort Carlton on June 15, 1858, also met wet weather—heavy rain on June 18, 20, 21 and 25, ("torrents" on June 18 and 20) with showers into July and incessant rain up to July 13.[66]

Bison and grasshoppers, early grazers

In July 1869, ten years before Macoun's visit, Isaac Cowie spent several days in the midst of a bison herd passing through Macoun's 'flower garden:' "[The bison] blackened the whole country, the compact, moving masses covering it so that not a glimpse of green grass could be seen....The earth trembled, day and night, as they moved in billow-like battalions over the undulations of the plain. Every drop of water on our way was foul and yellow with their wallowings and excretions. So we travelled among the multitude for several days." [67]

Grasshoppers also grazed the prairie, as noted by Henry Youle Hind, who encountered "hosts of grasshoppers....beyond all calculation" west of the Souris Sand Hills (near the present border with the U.S.) in early July, 1858. "Those portions of the prairie which had been visited by the grasshoppers wore a curious appearance: the grass was cut uniformly to one inch from the ground, and the whole surface was covered with the small, round, green exuviae of these destructive invaders."[68]

Herds of bison, historic grazers of the plains, were famous for their mud and dust wallows that created bare areas worked to a tilth and planted with seeds shed from their shaggy coats. A potential seed bed was there for invading.

Hind's grasshoppers were undoubtedly Rocky Mountain Locusts (*Melanoplus spretus*), whose swarms plagued the west in the latter part of the 1800s. These locusts razed the grassland like prairie fire: "The term *locust* is derived from the Latin, *locus ustus*, meaning 'burnt place'—an allusion to the denuded landscape left in the wake of a ravenous swarm. If we think of life being sustained by oxidative metabolism, the slow burn of biochemistry, then perhaps associating locusts with conflagration is remarkably appropriate. In a very real sense, a swarm of locusts is a metabolic wildfire burning tons of vegetation every day to fuel its migration." [69]

Ever-present fire

All travellers allude to the frequent prairie fires. Daniel Harmon wrote from near Good Spirit Lake on March 17, 1804, that "the country around us is all on fire." He adds that fires passed over the plains almost yearly.[70] Hind gives us an idea of the extent of some of the fires: "From beyond the South Branch of the Saskatchewan to Red River, all the prairies were burned last autumn [in 1857], a vast conflagration extended for one thousand miles in length and several hundreds in breadth. The dry season had so withered the grass that the whole country of the Saskatchewan was in flames....we traced the fire from the 49th parallel to the 53rd, and from the 98th to the 108th degree of longitude."[71] Macoun recommended burning prairie annually in spring "after the cattle have roamed over it all winter" to increase its value as pasture for cattle and horses, and noted that "Indians in past time burnt the grass over wide areas every fall, so that the young and tender grass of the burnt districts might tempt the buffalo to migrate."[72]

The prairies that inspired the Earl of Southesk and Macoun to marvel at masses of lilies appear to have been a wet, dynamic ecosystem, for at least some of the 20 years between 1858 and 1879. This was not to last; the prairies were on the brink of change. The Earl and Macoun were among the last to experience the Saskatchewan prairie as a wild, unbroken expanse left to the mercies of nature. Theirs was the pre-agricultural settlement period, which ended with the extirpation of the bison[73] and with the expansion of roads and the railway onto the prairies, beginning in the early 1880s.

"The term locust is derived from the Latin, locus ustus, meaning 'burnt place'—an allusion to the denuded landscape left in the wake of a ravenous swarm."

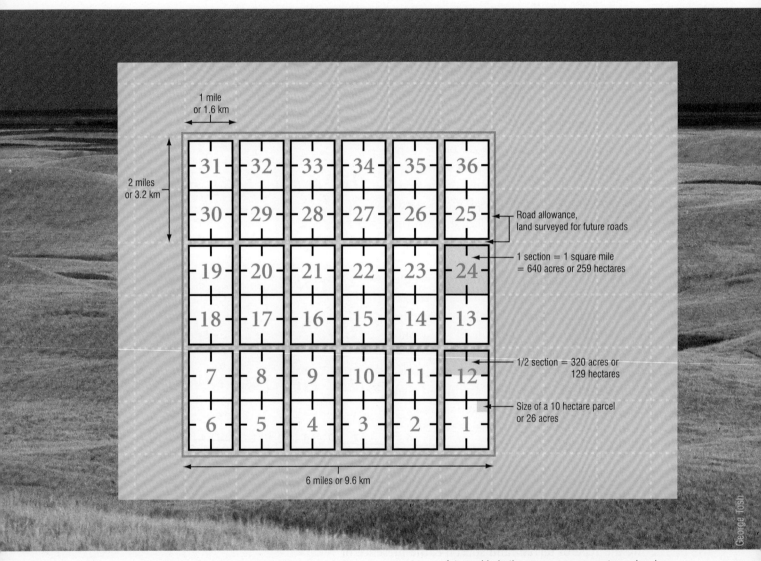

CHAPTER 8

1 mile
or 1.6 km

2 miles
or 3.2 km

31	32	33	34	35	36
30	29	28	27	26	25
19	20	21	22	23	24
18	17	16	15	14	13
7	8	9	10	11	12
6	5	4	3	2	1

Road allowance,
land surveyed for future roads

1 section = 1 square mile
= 640 acres or 259 hectares

1/2 section = 320 acres or
129 hectares

Size of a 10 hectare parcel
or 26 acres

6 miles or 9.6 km

George Tosh

A township in the square survey system, showing metric equivalents. One township contains 36 sections numbered in the sequence shown. The area of a township is 6 miles by 6 miles with 42 miles (67 km) of road allowance within each.

Agricultural settlement

Dividing the land into squares

The Dominion Land Survey was established in 1871 to survey the western territories of the Hudson Bay Company (Rupert's Land) which had become part of Canada in 1870. The survey was part of the federal government's plan to settle the west by making parcels of land available for homesteading.[74] This survey was a megaproject by any standard, and the process set in motion a style of land development that has altered the very fabric of the grassland and Aspen Parkland areas. The quantity of land surveyed was record-breaking.

Surveying the Grand Trunk Pacific Railway line between Melville and Yorkton, 1907.

As an example, about 11 million hectares were surveyed in connection with land grants to the Canadian Pacific Railway in 1883.[75] The system chosen was the square survey based on townships, each six miles square and containing 36 sections (each a square mile, 640 acres or approximately 259 hectares). Small groups of surveyors with horse, wagon, tent, surveyor chains (each 66 feet in length), range finders and transits or telescopic sighting devices traversed each section, noting the type of terrain and soil type, the presence of harvestable timber and the number and type of water bodies. They classified the land according to its suitability for agriculture and often commented on the weather, such as the frequent downpours that made their work difficult, and problems with horses and provisions which often cost time and wages. And they described the country they passed through. Surveyor M. J. Charbonneau wrote of the "luxuriant growth of grass," "snipe meadows covered with low stunted grass and salt weed" and "rolling prairie dotted with numerous sloughs" at the north end of Last Mountain Lake in 1883.[76]

A homesteader's camp near Alsask, ca 1910

....

In the mid-1880s the bison vanished, the Canadian Pacific Railway pushed across the west and treaties with the Plains Cree, Blackfoot and other First Nation groups were being forged. All of this put into motion the opening of this vast area to settlers, the practice of agriculture and the most incredible change—the breaking of the sod.

....

Alfred Langston plows on his homestead near Plunkett, in 1907.

....

Initially, as the engine of the agricultural machine was gaining momentum, the impact on the grassland ecosystem was limited. Although the land had been surveyed into a grid, native prairie still covered a vast expanse. Fires occurred frequently; in fact, fire incidence is thought to have increased during the time of first settlement due to new sources of ignition, such as railways and settlers.[77] Missing, however, were two important grazers: Rocky Mountain Locusts and bison. The absence of bison allowed prairie, kept short by grazing, to become tall enough to support a breeding population of Greater Prairie-Chickens at the beginning of the 20th century. This species, adapted to tall grass prairie, spread across Saskatchewan as far north as Lloydminster and Somme.[78] The thatch build-up resulting from the absence of bison may have also led to increasing severity of prairie fires when they did occur.

Lilies probably fared well during this transition period, for even without grazing by bison, fires provided a disturbance that kept the prairies close to their original, chaotic state. It was the 1930s' drought that precipitated a sharp decline in flowering populations of lilies and brought the need for conservation into focus. Changes set in motion 50 years earlier were having a profound effect. The land was drying out, blowing about with the wind, and some people began to question whether agricultural practices had upset the very 'balance of nature.'[79]

Lloyd T. Carmichael expressed the conservation sentiment of the time: "As a province and a nation, we have made many mistakes, recognizing to our sorrow only when it was too late. We have over-gunned the ducks, drained the swamps and then wondered why the game birds were disappearing; we have killed to the last bird the myriad passenger pigeons; we have slashed our forests with no thought of the future; we have turned valuable prairie land into a dust bowl; we have eliminated our natural buffalo population and have hunted to extinction species after species. Let us take the lesson, learned through lack of conservation to heart, and preserve our precious wild flowers."[80]

Taking stock in mid-century

The Red Lily was a focus of the conservation concern of the 1940s. The species was viewed as being crowded out of favoured habitat by ploughing of the land, dried out by loss of creeks and sloughs, and killed outright by heedless picking by pioneer families as they delighted in the brilliant flowers. In 1941, the 'prairie lily' was made the Saskatchewan floral emblem, a gesture that combined deep appreciation for the flower and an acute concern for its future.

In 1946, the Conservation Committee of the Regina Natural History Society sent questionnaires to about 600 'representative points' throughout the province to determine the species' status. The lily's ease of identification made it easy to assess whether it was becoming less widespread and less numerous, as many feared. The response to the survey was enthusiastic but not always encouraging. "From the following points comes the good news that [lilies] are actually increasing in numbers: Big River, Damour, Glen Elder, Kamsack, Kinistino, Le Roy, Loon Lake, Maryfield, Naicam, Nipawin, Okla, Porcupine Plain, Valley Centre, Wallwort, Windthorst, Wood Hill and Wroxton. On the other side of the picture comes the sad, passenger pigeon-like story of the realities of yesterday becoming only the dim recollections of today; places like Assiniboia, Bracken, Conquest, Glentworth, Gull Lake, Hawarden, Hazlet, Holdfast, Lawson, Meota, Mossbank, Traynor and Yellowgrass can only hope that the day will come again when our emblem will once more grace their roadsides and pastures. It is gratifying to learn that the lilies are not entirely absent from the south and southwest, and are growing at Portreeve, Carmichael, Gull Lake, Swift Current, Rush Lake, Neville, Old Wives, Tinley, Ormiston, Ogema, Big Beaver and Big Muddy."[81]

The general consensus after the survey was that there was a need to take measures to conserve this plant so that future generations could enjoy this 'rare beauty.' A public education program was launched primarily through the schools. For ten years following the survey, nature enthusiasts wrote to the Conservation Committee to comment on the relative abundance, or lack, of lilies and other wild flowers. The encouraging positive responses increased with moist years and waned with the dry. "A report received from Mrs. F. Bilsbury, Grenfell, seems typical of what took place in many districts. 'We have a spot on our farm,' she writes, 'where lilies grow. It is quite a large area on the west side of a big hay slough, lying between two clumps of trees. Part of the lily-covered land runs nearly into the slough. During the years 1919-1929 this spot of ground was a flaming mass of lilies. Then came the drought years and the lilies grew less and less until there was not one to be seen. However, to our great joy, in 1940 a few appeared in the old spot, increasing in numbers each season, and it is now [1945] a mass of bloom again.' "[82]

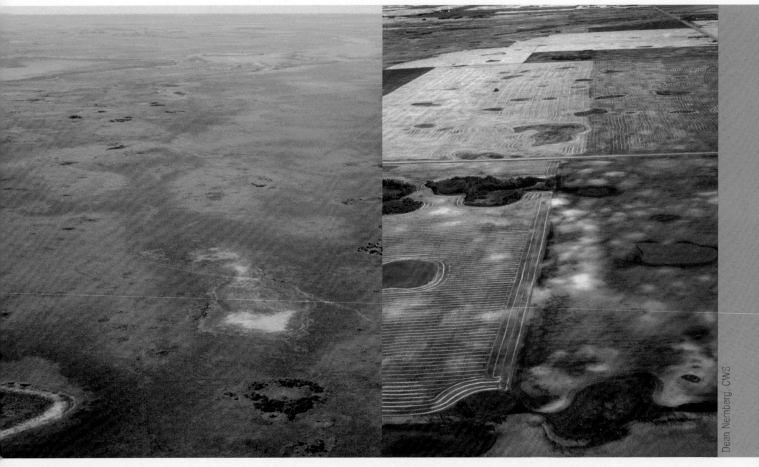

CHAPTER 9

Unbroken Prairie

Prairie fragments, in an agricultural grid

Dean Nernberg, CWS

The 21st century

Pushing cultivation to the limits

The drought of the 1930s caused people to consider what was happening to their immediate environment, but it didn't stop the breaking of land for agriculture. Loss of habitat for lilies—a concern in the 1950s—had become a fact by the end of the century. An example is the Regina Plain, one of the areas most modified today. This 9090 km² area was unbroken prairie 125 years ago. Now only 7% is native grassland; the majority is cropland and seeded pasture (88%), with 1% water and wetland, 1% tree and shrub and 3% other.[83] Loss of prairie habitat is not just a local phenomenon. Worldwide, temperate grasslands are one of the least protected, and most altered, ecosystems and this has certainly been the case in the Northern Great Plains.[84]

Large-scale loss of native prairie to land for cultivation slowed after the most productive lands for growing grain had been converted to cropland, but native prairie continued to be lost on a smaller scale. Existing fields were expanded to the edges of bluffs and sloughs; cities, highways and acreage developments grew exponentially; and the demand for sand and gravel for new roads removed cover from native areas too hilly or stony to cultivate.

Carpet fragments

For most of us, it is difficult to conjure up the Canadian North West at a time when the human footprint was small. "It is too bad that we cannot preserve memory for all time," laments Ben Bracegirdle, an early (1902) settler from the Last Mountain Lake area. He travelled the length and breadth of southern Saskatchewan (then the District of Assiniboia, North West Territories) around the turn of the century and in his mind's eye he could still see it as it was: "a great big garden, dotted with little lakes, very clean, and the lawn was always in nice shape. There were lots of flowers…scented with wolf willows, indescribably sweet and, in the low places, mint."[88] It is indeed a challenge to imagine a 650,000 km² carpet stretching from southeastern Alberta, across southern Saskatchewan and through parts of the Dakotas, Montana, Nebraska and Wyoming.[89]

GROW MORE GRAIN

With hunger in post-World-War-II Europe and other parts of the world, governments urged prairie farmers to increase grain production and feed the world. Farm mechanization had rendered superfluous draught animals and the 40-acre horse pasture on each farm. The Canadian Wheat Board quota system, which remained in place until the 1990s, tied the amount of grain each farmer could sell to the amount of cultivated land worked.[85] It was an agricultural policy that encouraged farmers to plough land considered marginal for agricultural, drain wetlands and convert native grassland into 'improved pasture.' In addition, land that was unimproved or left in a native state continued to be assessed for taxation purposes suggesting that such land should yield the owner some economic return.[86] Considering the economic and government pressure for increased productivity, it is amazing that any of the land especially suitable for agriculture still exists in an uncultivated state. In fact, in the prairie ecozone, only 2.1 % of the land with no, or only moderate, soil limitations for agriculture remains unbroken today.[87]

Today, this original prairie carpet lies in fragments. Although in Saskatchewan's three prairie ecoregions the total area in native vegetation—an estimated 48,079 km²—may seem large, most of this exists in small pieces. Only 1% of the land covered in native vegetation is in patches over 100 hectares in size, (less than a half section). Parcels smaller than this are numerous (122,549) but 95% of them are ten hectares or smaller. The Aspen Parkland, at the heart of the Red Lily's range in Saskatchewan, is the most fragmented of the three ecoregions: 96% of the area in native cover is in parcels smaller than 10 hectares (24,346 parcels). Size makes a big difference to the health of prairie remnants. Those smaller than 250 hectares (roughly one section or one square mile) will lose native species over time simply because of their small size.[90]

The advance of smooth brome grass into native grassland.

Fragmentation has brought unanticipated changes to native grasslands. The 1940s' concept of creating sanctuaries, "a refuge or a safe place" as described in Morrison's *The Prairie Lily*, to protect lilies has perhaps allowed us to expect more from prairie remnants than they are able to deliver. We have learned that many small fragments do not make a prairie. Small pieces of prairie, separated from each other by roads, settlements and cultivated land, are isolated from fires and the periodic impact of grazing. At the same time, these fragments are surrounded by established populations of invasive species planted in ditches and as forage throughout much the province. In many regions of the province, the most important of these invaders is smooth brome grass. It thrives in the absence of fire and grazing, and spreads by underground stems, as well as seeds, into native habitats, where it replaces native plants. These factors speed the loss of native species from prairie fragments.

Counting lilies in the 21st century

How have the lilies fared in the face of landscape changes in the last half century? In an attempt to find out, we invited people throughout the province to send us information on lily sightings in the year 2000. It was a fortunate choice of years. The preceding year was wet in much of the province, with the exception of the western edge, which was enduring a prolonged period of drought. In spite of relatively few responses from the southwest corner and along the west side of the province, we received over 300 sightings from the province as a whole.

THE BUILDING OF ROADS

Road building in the 20th century changed Saskatchewan from a landscape cut by trails and waterways to one crisscrossed by nearly 200,000 km of roads and highways—"more roads per capita than any other jurisdiction in the world."[91]

In 1883, John Macoun stated emphatically that "the truth is there are no roads in the country. What are familiarly called roads are merely trails used by buffalo hunters and Hudson's Bay Company employés when traversing the country from point to point."[92] A mere 40 years later in 1922, there were about 216,016 km (135,010 miles) of roads in the province: 16 km (10 miles) of gravel roads, 16,000 km (10,000 miles) of "improved" roads, and 200,000 km (125,000 miles) of "unimproved" roads.[93]

The survey system that divided the land into townships laid out roads in a grid with east-west roads every 2 miles and north-south roads at one mile intervals to "ensure easy communication from farm to market centre."[94] Not all of the roads set out were actually built, but if they had been, every 6 mile by 6 mile township would have been chopped into 18 rectangles, 1 mile wide and 2 miles high, each surrounded by six miles of road.

Fragmentation of the landscape by roads affected the spread of fires. As noted in 1915: "Although possibly as many fires take place as heretofore, yet the extent of the area burned over is not so large. This is doubtless due to the fact that whereas large tracts of land used to remain unbroken by road or fireguard, the country now is subdivided to such an extent that a fire is soon automatically stopped by its coming into contact with a road or similar obstruction." [95]

Saskatchewan Archives Board R-A 17758-2

Earth road leading down the east bank of the South Saskatchewan River Valley near Saskatoon in 1905.[96] "Some attempts have been made to improve them [road allowances] by building bridges over creeks and in some cases making a 'turnpike' by digging on either side of the road and throwing the earth into the centre. This when levelled makes a capital road in dry weather, but when it rains it is simply indescribable." John Macoun, *Manitoba and the Great North-West*, 1883. Did these early attempts to make a road out of the prairie dirt create the first ditch habitats for Red Lilies?

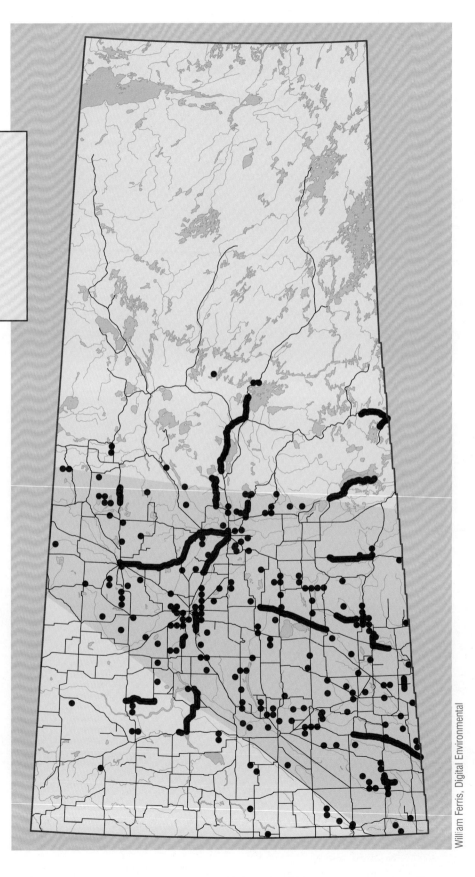

Point locations where survey participants saw lilies flowering in 2000.

Numerous patches of flowering lilies along roads and highways.

Portion of the province where the majority of the lilies were in the 1940s based on the results of the 1946 survey.

Locations of sightings from the year 2000 survey with the shaded area showing the centre of the lily range in 1946.

William Ferris, Digital Environmental

The range of the Red Lily has changed little in the last 50 years as shown in the map, opposite. The core of the species' range in Saskatchewan is a band running southeast to northwest across the province, centred on the Aspen Parkland. This was also the case as far back as collections go in Saskatchewan. Lilies do occur outside this area and the most striking change in the 50 years since the 1946 survey, is their expansion along highways built in the last three decades, heading north across the boreal plain. Lilies have long grown in the boreal forest, but what people reported in the year 2000 survey was the northward extension in roadside ditches. Sightings in ditches were not confined to the north; they occurred throughout the province and made up about half of the total number of reports that we received.

Why do lilies grow in ditches and how do they get there? Lilies move into ditches from adjacent land, for instance from a prairie remnant, as recounted by survey participant, Muriel Carlson: "Where two sections meet, a tiny triangle of land is preserved. Lilies have bloomed there for decades. As willows and shrubs grew, the lilies have been crowded out. Only one bloomed on the property in 2000. But 109 cascaded northwestward into the ditch, growing with grass, pussytoes, grass of Parnassus and blazing stars."

Lilies also travel along ditches once they get established there. An example is their northward spread along Highway 2 between Christopher Lake and La Ronge.

"The ditches on either side of Highway 2, between La Ronge and Waskesiu contain thousands of lilies....I noticed in August that the highway department had mown the ditches....I suspect that the mowing somehow enhances the lilies' spread. Having spent my boyhood in the Qu'Appelle Valley....we always checked a few special spots for Tiger Lilies, but I have never seen so many, so consistently, as in the ditches of Highway 2." – Rod Spooner, personal communication, 1997

Lilies flowering along the Hanson Lake road. The vegetation is sparse because the area was mowed to remove shrubs and young trees ('brushed').

Saskatchewan roadside ditches can provide lilies with almost ideal growing habitat: moist in spring but well-drained so that water does not stand in them throughout the summer. Seeds blown over snow may end up in ditches, where the relatively even moisture encourages germination and establishment. Lilies thrive in moist conditions and tolerate considerable disturbance, including regular mowing. Ditches should not be planted to smooth brome grass or treated with herbicides: lilies are crowded out by the former and killed outright by the latter.

Red Lilies often grow in scattered small groups in ditches along stretches of highway. One survey participant reported 32 separate groups ranging from 1 to "hundreds" along 50 km of Highway #1 from Wapella east to the Manitoba border—approximately 3,000 lilies in flower at the end of June 2000. Sometimes they bloom in astonishing masses, such as 16,000 estimated by survey participants to be growing in 22 km of ditch along Highway 120 north of Meath Park on July 9, 2000. In general, ditches adjacent to native areas such as pastureland or woods are much more likely to sport lilies that those beside cultivated land.

A return visit to Macoun's 'flower garden'

Are there still lilies in Macoun's 'Flower Garden of the North West?' Yes, and in some years the prairie is dotted with them. This area at the north end of Last Mountain Lake was reserved for Canada's first migratory bird sanctuary in 1887 (only eight years after Macoun's visit) and has been conserved as wildlife habitat for 118 years. Starting in the early 1980s, management practices have included controlled burning of natural grassland areas. In 1993, pulse grazing (intense grazing for short periods) was introduced over a wider area to combat invasive species such as smooth brome grass and to re-establish a natural ecosystem disturbance.

Some of the lilies in our study sites at the north end of the lake flower every year, with large numbers in good years. One such year was 1999, providing ample spring moisture to the native grassland that had been burned the previous spring and then grazed for two weeks in mid-July. We counted nearly 400 plants with flowers or buds in a 70 m by 10 m rectangle. These lilies neither "covered the ground bright red" as in Macoun's day, nor formed "intermingled masses" with harebells as described by the Earl of Southesk, but the sight was impressive. The bounty of flowering roses, smooth camas, harebells and lilies dominated the grasses, giving the overall appearance of a lush garden.

CWS

A controlled burn at Last Mountain Lake National Wildlife Area.

100

The future of the Red Lily

Conservation of the remaining scarce native grasslands deserves a great deal of public support. Roughly 70% is in private ownership; the rest is owned by government agencies or conservation organizations. It has been estimated that only about 20% of the remaining native prairie is in good shape as measured by the diversity of the plant community.[97]

"North American rangeland needs a consumer, we know that much. Protect a site from use for 15 years or so and it gets rank with dead material. Grass growth is restricted, snow mold becomes a problem, and soils stay cold far into the spring. We know the indigenous consumers were buffalo, grasshoppers, and fire, but we don't know how to replace them." – Don Gayton, *Wheatgrass Mechanism*, 1990

Like the Red Lily, the prairie depends on periodic disturbance events, such as fire, grazing, small mammal activity and even cycles of drought, to renew itself and maintain diversity. Restricting disturbance or even allowing the land to sit idle, permits the invasion of shrubs, trees, weeds and tame grasses. The rural road network has contributed to fragmentation of habitat in many areas and invasion of exotic species along the ditches. Clearly, managing the prairies for diversity is a complicated balancing act, but one that we must attend to if we want lilies to be a part of our landscape.

A PRESCRIPTION FOR LILIES

1. Honour the existing wild places. Consider that it is impossible to replace native habitat. If we want lilies then we will have to ensure that wetlands are not drained, marginal lands are not tilled or mined for sand and gravel, creek and river banks are protected, and urbanization and acreage development do not further erode the remnants of native prairie. Reward the farmer/landowner for maintaining native prairie. Route roads and railways around wetlands and unbroken areas, not straight through them.

2. Allow for disturbance events. Consider fire a source of renewal. Respect the need of small mammals to tunnel and churn the soil, but also the corresponding need for sufficient habitat to support their predators.

3. Eliminate future planting of invasive exotic plants for improved pasture and in road allowances. Implement programs to replace improved pasture and hay lands with native species.

4. Understand that to conserve the wild places where lilies grow is to preserve a vital part of ourselves—our cultural and spiritual well-being.

CHAPTER 10

Lilies viewing the world from a hilltop
north of Arcola.

Finding the lily

Lilies grow all around us, but finding them can be discouraging unless you know when and where to look. Knowing where to look is akin to knowing the best spots to pick wild berries. This chapter is intended to help you find flowering lilies near your home or in places you might visit in the province.

Where to look

Lilies grow in a surprising variety of disturbed and undisturbed habitats, including slough margins, shrubby and open upland sites, woods, under power lines and on railroad embankments. They do not grow on land that has been cultivated or in pastures planted to smooth brome grass and alfalfa.

Look for lilies on sites that are moist in spring but have sufficient drainage that the soil is not waterlogged throughout the growing season. Lilies often grow on hillsides or gentle slopes, but avoid the hottest and driest sites, such as south-facing slopes. They tolerate a wide range of light levels, from intense sun on the open grassland to light shade under the canopy of deciduous trees.

Lilies, smooth camas and wolf willow growing in a well vegetated roadside ditch east of Saskatoon.

Density of surface vegetation affects where lilies can grow: heavy thatch build-up on grassland sites prohibits establishment of seedlings, and slows or prevents spring emergence of established plants. Where thatch build-up might occur, look for lilies in areas that have been burned, hayed or mowed.

Lilies also grow in habitats with saline soils, such as slough margins and saline plains. These have largely been left in a native state because the soils are unproductive for crop use. Plants among which lilies grow in these habitats are wolf willow, smooth camas and saline shooting star. Lilies persist in wet areas such as slough margins even in dry years. Half of the 28 collections made in 1931 to 1950 and housed at the Fraser Herbarium at the University of Saskatchewan, came from wetlands: two near springs, two in river bottoms, one from a swamp, one from a low meadow, two from slough margins and six from saline meadows.

In upland areas, look for lilies in moist meadows (grazed or ungrazed), northeast-to-northwest-facing slopes, low sand hills, saline plains and gravel flats. Steep hillsides that have been spared from cultivation because of their slope, provide good habitat for lilies. Slopes offer lilies frost protection (cool air pools in low spots) as well as good air circulation and less humid conditions, thereby decreasing the risk of botrytis blight. Hillsides also attract butterflies, including swallowtails important in pollination. Something to look for on hillsides frequented by butterflies is a greater range of flower colour variation as a result of extensive cross-pollination by these insects.

This colourful array of sepals comes from eight different flowers within one population growing on a hillside in the boreal forest. Canadian Tiger Swallowtails actively pollinate the flowers at this site.

Wooded areas with lilies include aspen bluffs (though, in many, smooth brome grass has replaced the native understory), river valley slopes and the boreal forest, especially in woodland clearings and under aspen and birch in dappled sunlight. Nature trails in the Aspen Parkland and aspen-dominated pockets of the southern boreal forest feature a sprinkling of lilies along woods' edges.

With their taste for disturbance, Red Lilies can be found under power lines, along newly-upgraded rural roads and in logged areas, as noted by our survey participants in 2000. Railway embankments, which have been burned to keep weeds down, also provide habitat for lilies. F.W. Newth wrote "This afternoon, June 23, 1963, a young friend, Gary Seib, and I found Lady Slippers and Western Red Lilies in flower along the north side of the C.P.R. track at Jumping Deer Creek near here [Lipton]." [98]

RED LILIES AND THEIR ASSOCIATES IN SALINE AREAS

Vegetation detail showing plants typical of the alkali slough margin: wolf willow, smooth camas and Red Lily.

Lily habitat at the margin of an alkali slough.

Saline shooting star is another plant common in moist, alkali habitats. Its flowers arch forward and then open, like shooting stars, but later they turn their heads up and produce erect seed capsules.

The tall white spikes of smooth camas, another member of the lily family, are often seen with the Red Lily on moist sites.

UPLAND HABITATS FAVOURED BY RED LILIES

White sprays of northern bedstraw flowers accent
Red Lilies in moist meadows.

Axel Petersen, Saskatchewan Archives Board R-C7931

A sandy, juniper-covered slope along the South
Saskatchewan River south of Saskatoon.

A shrubby hillside facing northeast in the
Strawberry Hills east of Saskatoon.

When to look

The two-week period, July 1 to July 15, is designated 'Lily time' by Lloyd Carmichael in his delightful book, *Prairie Wildflowers*. "During these hot midsummer days there is a profusion of new blossoms to be found in every typical prairie habitat. Among some of the most cherished and spectacular wildflowers of this period are: Coneflower, on the open prairie; the flaming Western Red Lily, in the meadows; Fireweed, at the sides of the roads; and Pitcher Plants, in cool bogs. A host of others add their colours to the midsummer blaze."

The first half of July may be the most reliable time to find flowering lilies in Saskatchewan, but the plants begin to bloom in earnest the last week in June. About a quarter of the 170 flowering specimens from Saskatchewan and recorded in the W. P. Fraser Herbarium data base were collected between June 25 and June 30. This is slightly more than the number of specimens collected between July 3 and July 8, the other peak evident from this data base.

The first blooms appear well before the end of June, however. The dates of the earliest collections of flowering plants housed in this herbarium are June 3 (two plants in full flower at Fort à la Corne in 1980) and June 7 (one plant with three flowers and another with one, at Cranberry Flats, just south of Saskatoon, in 1994). From June 19 on, flowering specimens have been collected every day to almost the end of July. The latest collection of a plant in flower is August 1 (two plants near Prince Albert National Park in 1982).

> *"The hay areas (natural prairie) were normally cut about the second week in July when the lilies were usually reaching the end of blooming. The poem, 'Hay is made of flowers' comes to mind"*
>
> Earl Closson
> Survey participant
> Clair, 2000

Individual flowers last for six to nine days, but because not all individuals in a population come into bloom on the same date, a population of lilies stays in flower longer than that. We made daily observations in a lily population along a slough margin 20 km east of Saskatoon in 1999. Here the flowering period was about three weeks long. The first flower opened on June 27; the last, on July 18. The peak flowering period (when more than 50% of the population was in flower) occurred from July 9 to 14. These flowering times in 1999 were similar to those over a ten-year period at this location; most plants are in the late bud stages during our surveys in the first week of July.

Site characteristics can influence when a population will bloom. At our research plot in an upland meadow near Pike Lake, lilies flowered consistently earlier than those around the slough. More than 50% of the population was in flower in the upland meadow in the last week of June and the first week of July. Spring weather can also affect the date of first appearance of flowers. Cool

spring weather can delay the emergence of flower stalks from plants growing on wet ground. Once up and growing, however, these plants tend to catch up to those on drier sites and will flower within a few days of them. This trend was noted by Eugene Parfitt: "In Burnett county [Wisconsin] they blossom during the last week of June. Although the 1956 growing season was two weeks later than the 1955 season *L. philadelphicum* blossomed within three days of the same date both years."[99]

In sites where slope or aspect protects the plants from frost, the time of flowering is likely to be earlier than in low-lying wetland areas. There are often

A moist, west-facing slope along the riverbank south of Saskatoon. Paper birch and highbush cranberry share the hillside with the lilies.

A grassy opening under aspen poplar in the southern boreal forest.

Nature trail through mixed woods in Prince Albert National Park.

Detail of trailside vegetation showing spreading dogbane (white) and vetch (purple).

John Macoun's party "celebrated the 12th of July by decorating their horses with these lilies and marching from camp to the beat of the old tin pan."[101]

consistent yearly differences between lily patches with different site characteristics, even though the geographical location is similar.

In addition to site and yearly differences, there appear to be some regional trends in flowering time. In the grasslands of southern Saskatchewan, lilies seem to have a relatively short blooming period, with a distinct peak in the first week in July, whereas in the adjacent Aspen Parkland, the peak seems to be in the last week in June. Red Lilies in the boreal regions, while slower to start flowering, have a prolonged period of bloom, with good numbers still flowering at the end of July.

The summer solstice (about June 22) marks both the beginning of summer and widespread flowering of lilies in Saskatchewan. If you start to watch for flowers on the solstice, you may catch the first ones opening and you will see the whole population come into bloom over a few weeks. Letting lilies mark the beginning of our prairie summer adds truth to Henry David Thoreau's words of July 9, 1852: "The red lily, with its torrid color and sun-freckled spots, dispensing, too, with the outer garment of a calyx, its petals so open and wide apart that you can see through it in every direction, tells of hot weather.... It belongs not to spring." [100]

A flower of summer

George Tosh

EPILOGUE

Over the past 50 years, local attitudes toward the Red Lily have changed. Saskatchewan residents once freely picked the flowers, confident in their abundance; now, if they pick at all, it is with a guilty conscience. Changes in how and where prairie people live have been partly responsible for this shift in attitudes; provincial legislation protecting the plant also has helped. Although not put in place until 1981, *The Floral Emblem Act* arose from concerns expressed in the '50s, '60s and '70s by provincial natural history societies about uncontrolled picking. The law reads: "No person shall pick, cut down, dig, pull up, injure or destroy, in whole or in part, whether in blossom or not, the plant that produces the flower that is the floral emblem of Saskatchewan."

Whereas the *Act*, and its successor in 1988, prohibit injury and destruction to individual plants by pickers, they make no provision for the protection of the lily, or lily habitat, by those whose livelihoods infringe upon where lilies live: road builders, landowners and developers. In fact, the law specifically exempts "persons engaged in the lawful carrying out of any public work or of his occupation; or the carrying out of necessary work on property owned or lawfully occupied by him." As the native habitat that supports lilies in all corners of the prairies becomes more endangered than the plant itself, the protection granted against picking seems inadequate at best.

In the face of current conservation concerns that focus on habitat loss, it may be time to shake off nostalgic feelings about the lily as an emblem and ask ourselves how important the Red Lily is to us as a living, growing entity. If we do care about this native Saskatchewan wild flower, we will do well to direct our attention to where and how it grows. To survive, wild flowers require a place within natural communities. To ensure that the Red Lily will be a part of the Saskatchewan landscape for generations to come, individuals as well as governments need to do everything in their power to husband the province's remnant natural landscapes. We have embraced the Red Lily as the emblem; we also hold its fate in our hands.

Our lily is unsurpassed for its bright beauty, admired for its resilience in a climate known for extremes of temperature and drought, and found in a diversity of habitats throughout a wide geography. It is easy to assume that this is a plant that will endure from generation to generation. And yet its future is not assured. To keep the Red Lily as a living, enduring part of our natural heritage, and not just a part of our past, will take courage, bold initiatives and perseverance.

We have a symbol for that.

ACKNOWLEDGEMENTS

Throughout our study and the writing of this book, the generosity of people in contributing advice, equipment, photography and logistical support has been tremendous.

Jim Sullivan, lily grower and enthusiast, has been a valued source of information and insight and a contributor to many discussions. He has also made his photographs available to us for use in this book and other publications associated with the study. As an artist, he has brought his keen observations to the watercolour on the frontispiece, reproduced as a miniature, opposite. He also provided the watercolour images on the title page of Parts 1-3 and the inside covers.

Taylor Steeves has been a mentor from the very beginning, introducing us to his world of microtomes and plant structure, as well as sharing the knowledge he gained from his research into how wild plants work. His advice and role in facilitating the field and laboratory investigations were essential.

The Biology Department at the University of Saskatchewan provided more than a nurturing environment for our young plants. Jeaniene Smith welcomed the lilies entrusted to her care at the Biology Department greenhouse, Art Davis and Thurston Lacalli assisted by providing space and access to equipment in their labs, and Dennis Dyck helped with photography.

Other people at the University of Saskatchewan have also given us valuable assistance: Jim Germida provided equipment and lab space for the mycorrhizal study; Bohdan Pylypec loaned us field equipment; Vern Harms and Bob Redmann provided early advice and encouragement; Judy Haraldson and Randy Olson compiled information on collections housed in the W. P. Fraser Herbarium; Ian Shirley helped us photograph the thrips and Elise Pietroniro of the Geography Department provided ready assistance with maps published in the Atlas of Saskatchewan.

We have relied on experts from Saskatchewan and Alberta to identify insects: Bruce Hemming (thrips), Dan Johnson (bush katydid), Ron Hooper, Ken Pivnick and Greg Pohl (moths). Bruce Gossen confirmed our initial identification of botrytis blight and provided information on the disease.

Nature Saskatchewan provided early financial support for the study through its Members Initiative Grant. Friends of the Environment, the Regina Prairie Garden Group and the Canadian Prairie Lily Society also assisted with funding. We were grateful to receive two grants from the Saskatchewan Heritage Foundation for our study in natural history.

The wonderful staff at the Last Mountain Lake National Wildlife Area provided logistical support, a home away from home, and have made our work there a pleasure. Special thanks to John Dunlop, Lois Vanthuyne, Ken Born, Ron Kennedy, Kerry Hecker, Dean Nernberg and Philip Taylor. We are grateful for the continuous support that the Canadian Wildlife Service has given this research project since 1995.

In the year 2000, we asked the general public to respond to a survey of lily sightings around the province and we received an enthusiastic reply. We greatly appreciate the generosity of all those who took time to send us information, personal anecdotes and photographs.

Nature Saskatchewan provided access to its website for distribution of information about the year 2000 survey and Heather Trueman designed the survey web pages.

We wish to thank the following people for reading an early draft of the book and providing valuable editorial comments: Alice Doerr, Mary Gilliland, Vern Harms, Mary and Stuart Houston, Ted Leighton, Frank Roy, Allan Safarik, Taylor and Peggy Steeves, and Philip Taylor.

Many people have contributed photographs to the book: Viola Coutu, Robert E. Gehlert, Laura Herman, Brian Irving, Shirley Johnston, John Kozial, Dean Nernberg, Donna Stang, Nora Stewart, Jim Sullivan, Philip Taylor, George Tosh and Roy Whitely. A number of photographs used in the book came from the Regina and Saskatoon branches of Saskatchewan Archives. The helpful staff at both these offices provided a wonderful service. We also thank the staff at the Saskatoon Public Library's Local History Room for looking for materials on lilies for us and George Kovalenko for providing information on the archival photograph of Saskatoon.

For preparation of the figures in the book, we relied on the considerable expertise of several people. George Tosh devoted many hours to scanning and preparing slides, prints and negatives for this book. William Ferris at Digital Environmental generously assisted our project by mapping lily locations received from survey participants and produced the map on page 98. The map at the bottom of page 14 was designed by Elise Pietroniro originally for the CD Rom version of the Atlas of Saskatchewan. Tom Reaume provided the drawings of the Red Lily on page 20 and 29, as well as several of those on page 37. (The other Red Lily and animal drawings were done by Bonnie Lawrence.)

Other people we thank are Robin and Arlene Karpan for their advice on book publishing; George Swerhone for his helpful advice and assistance in preparing graphics and photo-imaging; Micheline B.-Bouchard at the Canadian Museum of Nature, who searched through specimens housed in the National Herbarium in Ottawa for information on lily collections from Churchill, Manitoba; Lorne Duczek, who spent time on his vacation in Churchill in 2004 to look for lilies and note details of their distribution; and Victor Friesen for tracking down quotations by Thoreau cited in this book.

We are grateful for the support of many people who showed interest in the lily project over the years and who provided encouragement in myriad ways.

Finally, we thank our families for support during the decade that this project has been our preoccupation.

ENDNOTES

1. The phrase 'flight of the scarlet lilies' was used by Georgina Binnie-Clark in *A Summer on the Canadian Prairie*. It speaks to the brevity and synchrony of the flowering season in a patch or 'flock' of lilies.

2. Belcher, M. 1996. The Isabel Priestly Legacy. Special Publication No. 19, Nature Saskatchewan, Regina.

3. The written sources of information that provided the basis for the distribution of *Lilium philadelphicum* and its varieties are listed in a separate list at the end of the references. Churchill perhaps should have been left off the range map due to uncertainty about its current status. It is included on the basis of a comment about distribution in the *Flora of Canada* (Scoggan 1978, p. 500) "? intro. along a railway from Gillam to as far N as Churchill." At the request of the authors, members of a University of Saskatchewan nature tour to Churchill in early July 2004 looked for Red Lilies along the railroad as they travelled by train north from The Pas, Manitoba. They saw lilies blooming on both sides of the railroad as far north as Thicket Portage (about 60 km south of Thompson) and none was seen north of that point. A local woman on the train stated that they did not grow north of Thompson, Manitoba. None was seen by the Saskatchewan naturalists in the Churchill area and no records of lilies were known to local botanists familiar with the plants of the area.

4. Woodcock, H. B. D. and W. T. Stearn. 1950. Lilies of the World: Their Cultivation and Classification. Charles Scribner's Sons, New York.

5. Pennell, F. W. 1936. Travels and scientific collections of Thomas Nuttall. *Bartonia* 18:1-51. Pennell's date for Nuttall's visit to Fort Mandan differs from that given by Woodcock and Stern (1950, p. 309), who give the date as June 1812.

6. Shaw, C. C. 1948. [Note] *Blue Jay* 6 (2):31.

7. Francis, C. S. 1950. [Note] *Blue Jay* 8 (3):26.

8. Raup, H. M. 1934. Phytogeographical studies in the Peace and Upper Liard river regions, Canada, with a catalogue of the vascular plants. Contributions of the Arnold Arboretum of Harvard University, No. VI. Jenkins Lake is located between Lac la Biche and Slave Lake.

9. Synge, P. M. 1980. Lilies: A Revision of Elwes' Monograph of the Genus *Lilium* and its Supplements. Universe Books, New York, p. 185.

10. Priestly, I. M. 1945. Report on the Western Red Lily. *Blue Jay* 4 (1):2.

11. Richards, B. 1968. Record Lily. *Blue Jay* 26 (1):61.

12. Thacker, C. 1953. A Remarkable Lily. *Blue Jay* 11 (3):18.

13. Sullivan, J. 1991. A Lily of the Canadian Prairies. *The Lily Yearbook of the North American Lily Society* 44: 82-83, p. 83.

14. Torrey, B. and F. H. Allen (eds.) 1962. (Dover Edition) The Journal of Henry D. Thoreau. Volumes 1 & 2. Dover Publications, New York, p.1032. This quotation appears on page 409 of Volume 8 of Thoreau's original journal.

15. Barrows, E. M. 1979. Flower biology and arthropod associates of *Lilium philadelphicum*. The Michigan Botanist 18 (3):109-115; Edwards, J. and J. R. Jordan. 1992. Reversible anther opening in *Lilium philadelphicum* (Liliaceae): a possible means of enhancing male fitness. *American Journal of Botany* 79 (2): 144-148.

16. Barrows, E. M. 1979. Flower biology and arthropod associates of *Lilium philadelphicum*. *The Michigan Botanist* 18 (3):109-115; Skinner, M. W. 2002. *Lilium*. In: Flora of North America Editorial Committee (ed.)

Magnoliophyta: Liliidae: Liliales and Orchidales. Volume 26. Flora of North America North of Mexico, Oxford University Press, New York, p. 172-197.

17. Grant, K. A. and V. Grant. 1968. Hummingbirds and Their Flowers. Columbia University Press, New York.

18. Olson, J. 1991. Native Lily Conservation in Wisconsin. *The Lily Yearbook of the North American Lily Society* 44:74-78. p. 76.

19. Skinner, M. W. 2002. Lilium. In: Flora of North America Editorial Committee (ed.) Magnoliophyta: Liliidae: Liliales and Orchidales. Volume 26. Flora of North America North of Mexico, Oxford University Press, New York, pp. 172-197.

20. Barrows, E. M. 1979. Flower biology and arthropod associates of *Lilium philadelphicum. The Michigan Botanist* 18 (3):109-115.

21. Edwards, J. and J. R. Jordan. 1992. Reversible anther opening in *Lilium philadelphicum* (Liliaceae): a possible means of enhancing male fitness. *American Journal of Botany* 79 (2): 144-148.

22. Edwards, J. and J. R. Jordan. 1992. Reversible anther opening in *Lilium philadelphicum* (Liliaceae): a possible means of enhancing male fitness. *American Journal of Botany* 79 (2): 144-148.

23. Skinner, M. W. 2002. Lilium. In: Flora of North America Editorial Committee (ed.) Magnoliophyta: Liliidae: Liliales and Orchidales. Volume 26. Flora of North America North of Mexico, Oxford University Press, New York, pp. 172-197.

24. Woodcock, H. B. D. and W. T. Stearn. 1950. Lilies of the World: Their Cultivation and Classification. Charles Scribner's Sons, New York, p. 26.

25. Sources of information for the text box on First Nations' lore and uses are Hellson, J. C. and M. Gadd. 1974. Ethnobotany of the Blackfoot Indians. Canadian Ethnology Service Paper No. 19. National Museums of Canada, Ottawa (Blackfoot names and uses); Scott-Brown, J. M. 1977. Stoney Ethnobotany: An Indication of Cultural Change Amongst Stoney Women at Morley, Alberta. Master's Thesis, University of Calgary (Assiniboine uses); Gilmore, M. R. 1919. Uses of Plants by the Indians of the Missouri River Region. 33rd Annual Report, Bureau of American Ethnology, Smithsonian Institution, Washington, D.C. (Dakota uses); Moerman, D. E., 2002. Native American Ethnobotany. Timber Press, Portland, Oregon (medicinal properties). The quotation in this text box is from Gilmore 1919, p. 71.

26. Woodcock, H. B. D. and W. T. Stearn. 1950. Lilies of the World: Their Cultivation and Classification. Charles Scribner's Sons, New York, p. 25.

27. Rockwell, F. F., E. C. Grayson and J. de Graaf. 1961. The Complete Book of Lilies. Doubleday & Company, Garden City, New York.

28. Olson, J. 1991. Native Lily Conservation in Wisconsin. *The Lily Yearbook of the North American Lily Society* 44, pp. 74-77.

29. Richardson, J. 1823. Botanical Appendix. In: Franklin, John. Narrative of a Journey to the Polar Sea in the Years 1819-20-21-22. John Murray, London. pp. 729-763, p.735.

30. Banfield, A. W. F. 1974. The Mammals of Canada. University of Toronto Press, Toronto, p. 211.

31. Banfield, A. W. F. 1974. The Mammals of Canada. University of Toronto Press, Toronto.

32. Kindscher, K. 1987. Edible Wild Plants of the Prairie. University of Kansas Press, Lincoln, Kansas.

33. Gilmore, M. R. 1919. Uses of Plants by the Indians of the Missouri River Region. 33rd Annual Report, Bureau of American Ethnology, Smithsonian Institution, Washington, D.C., p. 96.

34. Banfield, A. W. F. 1974. The Mammals of Canada. University of Toronto Press, Toronto.

35. Sources of information for the text box on the Meadow Vole are Banfield, A. W. F. 1974. The Mammals of Canada. University of Toronto Press, Toronto; Hoffmeister, D. 1989. Mammals of Illinois. University of Illinois Press, Champaign, IL; Jackson, H. H. T. 1961. Mammals of Wisconsin. University of Wisconsin Press, Madison, WI.; Seton, E. T. 1909. Life-histories of Northern Animals. Volume 1: Grass Eaters. C. Scribner's Sons, New York.

36. Sources of information for the text box on the Prairie Vole are Banfield, A. W. F. 1974. The Mammals of Canada. University of Toronto Press, Toronto; Criddle, S. 1926. Habits of *Microtus minor* in Manitoba. *Journal of Mammology* 7(3):193-200; Hoffmeister, D. 1989. Mammals of Illinois. University of Illinois Press, Champaign, IL; Jackson, H. H. T. 1961. Mammals of Wisconsin. University of Wisconsin Press, Madison, WI.; Seton, E. T. 1909. Life-histories of Northern Animals. Volume 1: Grass Eaters. C. Scribner's Sons, New York.

37. Criddle, S. 1947. *Microtus minor* and the Prairie Lily. *Canadian Field-Naturalist* 61:116.

38. Sources of information for the text box on the Northern Pocket Gopher are Banfield, A. W. F. 1974. The Mammals of Canada. University of Toronto Press, Toronto; Criddle, S. 1930. The Prairie Pocket Gopher, *Thomomys talpoides rufescens. Journal of Mammology* 11(3):265-280; Salt, J. R. 1976. Seasonal food and prey relationships of badgers in east-central Alberta. *Blue Jay* 34(2):119-122. The quotation is from Banfield, 1974, p. 148.

39. Rockwell, F. F., E. C. Grayson and J. de Graaf. 1961. The Complete Book of Lilies. Doubleday & Company, Garden City, New York, p. 73.

40. Synge, P. M. 1980. Lilies: A Revision of Elwes' Monograph of the Genus *Lilium* and its Supplements. Universe Books, New York.

41. Sullivan, J. 1991. A Lily of the Canadian Prairies. *The Lily Yearbook of the North American Lily Society* 44: 82-83.

42. Fitter, A. H. and J. W. Merryweather. 1992. Why are some plants more mycorrhizal than others? An ecological inquiry. In: Read, D. J., D. H. Lewis, A. H. Fitter and I. J. Alexander (eds.). Mycorrhizas in Ecosystems. C-A-B International, Wallingford, UK. pp. 26-36.

43. Currah, R. S. and M. van Dyk. 1986. A survey of some perennial vascular plant species native to Alberta for occurrence of mycorrhizal fungi. *The Canadian Field-Naturalist* 100(3): 330-342.

44. Shaw, C. C. 1947. General Notes. *Blue Jay* 6 (1): 8.

45. Schuster, J. 2001. Botrytis (gray mold): a disease for many plants. http://www.urbanext.uiuc.edu/hortihints (Accessed August 18, 2004).

46. Synge, P. M. 1980. Lilies: A Revision of Elwes' Monograph of the Genus *Lilium* and its Supplements. Universe Books, New York, p. 235.

47. Ende, J. E. van den and M. G. Pennock-Vos, 1997. Primary sources of inoculum of *Botrytis elliptica* in lily. Acta Horticulturae. Volume 2. Issue 430: 591-595.

48. Archibold, O. W., L. J. Nelson, E. A. Ripley and L. Delanoy. 1998. Fire temperature in plant communities of the northern mixed prairie. *The Canadian Field-Naturalist* 112 (2):234-240.

49. Archibold, O. W., E. A. Ripley and L. Delanoy. 2003. Effects of season of burning on the microenvironment of fescue prairie in central Saskatchewan. *The Canadian Field-Naturalist* 117 (2):257-266.

50. Drysdale, P. D. (ed.) 1983. Gage Canadian Dictionary. Gage Publishing Limited, Toronto, p. 848.

51. Vogl, R. J. 1974. Effects of Fire on Grasslands. In: Kozlowski, T. T. (ed.) Fire and Ecosystems. Academic Press, New York, pp. 139-194.

52. Savage, C. 2004. Prairie, A Natural History. Greystone Books, Vancouver.

53. Bagyaraj, D. J. 1991. Ecology of vesicular arbuscular mycorrhizae. In: Arora, D. K. *et al.* (eds.) Handbook of Applied Mycology. Volume 1: Soils and Plants. Marcel Dekker Inc., New York, pp. 3-34.

54. Driver, E. A. 1987. Fire on grasslands—friend or foe? *Blue Jay* 45 (4): 217-225.

55. Silcox, D and V. L. Harms. 1989. The yellow immaculate lily in Saskatchewan and adjacent Manitoba, and its persistence in native lily patches. *Blue Jay* 47 (2): 69-73, pp. 71 & 72.

56. Priestly, I. M. 1945. Report on the Western Red Lily. *Blue Jay* 4 (1):2.

57. Boon, E. C. 1952. Flowers in profusion. *Blue Jay* 10 (3):24.

58. Leighton, A. 2000. Buzzing ball baffles botanist. *Blue Jay* 58(2):104.

59. Southesk, The Earl of (James Carnegie). 1875. Saskatchewan and The Rocky Mountains. Edmonston and Douglas, Edinburgh, p. 70.

60. Macoun, J. 1979 (1922). Autobiography of John Macoun, M.A., Second Edition. Ottawa Field Naturalists' Club, Ottawa, p. 141.

61. Macoun, J. 1895. 'J. Macoun to Hon. T. M. Daly, November 21, 1889.' Canada Department of the Interior, File Number 123293. In: Raby, S. 1966. Prairie fires in the north-west. *Saskatchewan History* XIX (3): 81-99, pp. 94-99.

62. Macoun, J. 1883. Manitoba and the Great North-West. Thomas C. Jack, London.

63. Macoun, J. 1895. 'J. Macoun to Hon. T. M. Daly, November 21, 1889.' Canada Department of the Interior, File Number 123293. In: Raby, S. 1966. Prairie Fires in the North-west. *Saskatchewan History* XIX (3): 81-99, pp. 94-99.

64. Macoun, J. 1883. Manitoba and the Great North-West. Thomas C. Jack, London, p. 171.

65. Southesk, The Earl of (James Carnegie). 1875. Saskatchewan and The Rocky Mountains. Edmonston and Douglas, Edinburgh.

66. Spry, I. M. (ed.) 1968. The Papers of the Palliser Expedition 1857-1860. The Champlain Society, Toronto, p. 53.

67. Cowie, I. 1913. The Company of Adventurers. William Briggs, Toronto, pp. 373-374.

68. Hind, H. Y. 1971 [1860]. Narrative of the Canadian Red River Exploring Expedition of 1857 and of the Assiniboine and Saskatchewan Exploring Expedition of 1858. Volume I. Originally published by Charles E. Tuttle Company, Vermont. Reprinted by M. G. Hurtig, Edmonton, p. 298.

69. Lockwood, J. A. 2004. Locust. Basic Books, New York. The locust mysteriously disappeared just after the turn of the century but several related species of grasshoppers continued the tradition of forming destructive hoards in drought years across the prairie region, p. 26-27.

70. Lamb, W. K. 1957, Sixteen Years in the Indian Country: The Journal of Daniel Williams Harmon, 1800-1816. MacMillan Company, Toronto, p. 77.

71. Hind, H. Y. 1971 [1860]. Narrative of the Canadian Red River Exploring Expedition of 1857 and of the Assiniboine and Saskatchewan Exploring Expedition of 1858. Volume I. Originally published by Charles E. Tuttle Company, Vermont. Reprinted by M. G. Hurtig, Edmonton, p. 292.

72. Macoun, J. 1883. Manitoba and the Great North-West. Thomas C. Jack, London, pp. 238-239.

73. Roe, F. G. 1970. The North American Buffalo. Second Edition. University of Toronto Press, Toronto. The large herds of bison had left Saskatchewan by 1879 but isolated small groups persisted in the western parts of the province into the mid-1880s.

74. Lalond, A. N. and M. A. Pedersen. 1999. Administration of Dominion Lands 1870-1930. In: Fung, K. (ed.) Atlas of Saskatchewan. University of Saskatchewan, Saskatoon, pp. 48-49.

75. Lajeunesse, C. 1996. Surveying. In: Canadian Encyclopaedia Plus (CD rom version), McClelland and Stewart, Toronto.

76. White, T. (ed.) 1886. Descriptions of the Townships of the North-west Territories. MacLean Roger & Co., Ottawa, p. 241.

77. Raby, S. 1966. Prairie fires in the northwest. *Saskatchewan History* 19:81-99.

78. Houston, C. S. 2002. Spread and disappearance of the Greater Prairie-Chicken, *Tympanuchus cupido*, on the Canadian prairies and adjacent areas. *The Canadian Field-Naturalist* 116 (1):1-21.

79. Morrison, D. 1948. The Prairie Lily. School Aids and Text Book Publishing Company, Ltd, Regina, p. 13.

80. Carmichael, L. T. 1945. Saskatchewan's own lilies. *Blue Jay* 3 (4):32

81. Carmichael, L. T. 1946. Report on the Red Lily by the Conservation Committee, Regina Natural History Society. *Blue Jay* 4 (3):27-28.

82. Priestly, I. M. 1945. Report on the Western Red Lily. *Blue Jay* 4 (1):2.

83. Hammermeister, A. M, D. Gauthier and K. McGovern. 2001. Saskatchewan's Native Prairie: Taking stock of a vanishing ecosystem and dwindling resource. Native Plant Society of Saskatchewan, Saskatoon.

84. World Wildlife Website. The nature audit, Part II: Grassland habitat accounts. http://wwf.ca/About WWF/ What We Do/ The Nature Audit/The Nature Audit. (Accessed January 2004.)

85. Thornton, F., J. Bowman and D. Struthers. 1993. Agricultural policy review part 2: Wheat Board Quota System. *Blue Jay* 51(2):65-71.

86. Sawatzky, H. L. 1979. Prairie potholes. *Blue Jay* 37(1):3-8.

87. Hammermeister, A. M, D. Gauthier and K. McGovern. 2001. Saskatchewan's Native Prairie: Taking stock of a vanishing ecosystem and dwindling resource. Native Plant Society of Saskatchewan, Saskatoon.

88. Bracegirdle, B. 1980. [recollections] In: Last Mountain Echoes. Govan and District Local History Association, Govan, SK, p. 210.

89. World Wildlife Website. The nature audit, Part II: Grassland habitat accounts. http://wwf.ca/About WWF/ What We Do/ The Nature Audit/The Nature Audit. (Accessed January 2004.)

90. Hammermeister, A. M, D. Gauthier and K. McGovern. 2001. Saskatchewan's Native Prairie: Taking stock of a vanishing ecosystem and dwindling resource. Native Plant Society of Saskatchewan, Saskatoon.

91. Barry, B., V. Gooliaff and R. Reid. 1999. Development of Transportation. In: Fung, K. (ed.) Atlas of Saskatchewan. University of Saskatchewan, Saskatoon, p. 261.

92. Macoun, J. 1883. Manitoba and the Great North-West. Thomas C. Jack, London, p. 288.

93. Nader, G. A. and W. K. Setter. 1969. Transportation in Saskatchewan. In: Richards, J. H. and K. I. Fung (eds.) Atlas of Saskatchewan. University of Saskatchewan, Saskatoon, p. 174.

94. Nader, G. A. and W. K. Setter. 1969. Transportation in Saskatchewan. In: Richards, J. H. and K. I. Fung (eds.) Atlas of Saskatchewan. University of Saskatchewan, Saskatoon, p. 174.

95. Canada, Sessional Papers, 1916, Vol. 51, No. 28, p. 68 cited in Raby, S. 1966. Prairie fires in the northwest. *Saskatchewan History* 19:81-99, p. 91.

96. The dirt road is in the approximate location of the current Eastlake Avenue. The white house visible on the opposite bank is at 414 Spadina Crescent East.

97. Hammermeister, A. M, D. Gauthier and K. McGovern. 2001. Saskatchewan's Native Prairie: Taking stock of a vanishing ecosystem and dwindling resource. Native Plant Society of Saskatchewan, Saskatoon.

98. Heath, F. W. 1963. Lady Slippers. *Blue Jay* 21 (4):163. "Heath" appears to be a misspelling of the name Newth. The man who accompanied Gary on the outing mentioned in this note was F. W. Newth, (Gary Seib, pers. comm., 2004).

99. Parfitt, E. E. 1957. *Lilium philadelphicum* in Wisconsin. *The Lily Yearbook of the North American Lily Society* 10: 76-77.

100. Torrey, B. and F. H. Allen (eds.) 1962. (Dover Edition). The Journal of Henry D. Thoreau. Volumes 1 & 2. Dover Publications, New York, p. 452. This quotation occurs on pages 406-407 in Volume 4 of Thoreau's original journal.

101. Macoun, J. 1979 (1922). Autobiography of John Macoun, M.A. Second Edition. Ottawa Field Naturalists' Club, Ottawa, p. 315.

REFERENCES CITED

Archibold, O. W., L. J. Nelson, E. A. Ripley and L. Delanoy. 1998. Fire temperature in plant communities of the northern mixed prairie. *The Canadian Field-Naturalist* 112 (2):234-240.

Archibold, O. W., E. A. Ripley and L. Delanoy. 2003. Effects of season of burning on the microenvironment of fescue prairie in central Saskatchewan. *The Canadian Field-Naturalist* 117 (2):257-266.

Bagyaraj, D. J. 1991. Ecology of vesicular arbuscular mycorrhizae. In: Arora, D. K. et al. (eds.) Handbook of Applied Mycology. Volume 1: Soils and Plants. Marcel Dekker Inc., New York, pp. 3-34.

Banfield, A. W. F. 1974. The Mammals of Canada. University of Toronto Press, Toronto.

Barrows, E. M. 1979. Flower biology and arthropod associates of *Lilium philadelphicum*. *The Michigan Botanist* 18 (3): 109-115.

Barry, B., V. Gooliaff and R. Reid. 1999. Development of Transportation. In: Fung, K. (ed.) Atlas of Saskatchewan. University of Saskatchewan, Saskatoon, p. 261.

Belcher, M. 1996. The Isabel Priestly Legacy. Special Publication No. 19, Nature Saskatchewan, Regina.

Binnie-Clark, G. 1910. A Summer on the Canadian Prairie. Musson Book Company, Toronto.

Boon, E. C. 1952. Flowers in profusion. *Blue Jay* 10 (3):24.

Bracegirdle, B. 1980. [recollections] In: Last Mountain Echoes. Govan and District Local History Association, Govan, SK, p. 211.

Bray, T. H. and H. Newton. 1955. Nature 1904-1955. *Blue Jay* 13(2):15.

Brown, A. R. 1955. Prairie Lily hybrids. *The Lily Yearbook of the North American Lily Society* 8: 94-95.

Canada, Sessional Papers, 1916, Vol. 51, No. 28, p. 68 cited in Raby 1966, p. 91.

Carmichael, L. T. 1945. Saskatchewan's own lilies. *Blue Jay* 3 (4):32.

Carmichael, L. T. 1946. Report on the Red Lily by the Conservation Committee, Regina Natural History Society. *Blue Jay* 4 (3):27-28.

Carmichael, L. T. 1947. Botany. *Blue Jay* 5 (3 & 4):33.

Carmichael, L. T. 1961. Prairie Wildflowers. J. M. Dent & Sons, Toronto. Quotation cited is on page 105.

Costello, D. F. 1969. The Prairie World. Thomas Y. Crowell, N. Y. The quotation cited is on page 194.

Cowie, I. 1913. The Company of Adventurers. William Briggs, Toronto.

Criddle, S. 1926. Habits of *Microtus minor* in Manitoba. *Journal of Mammology* 7(3):193-200.

Criddle, S. 1930. The Prairie Pocket Gopher, *Thomomys talpoides rufescens*. *Journal of Mammology* 11(3):265-280. Quotation cited is on pages 274-275.

Criddle, S. 1947. *Microtus minor* and the Prairie Lily. *The Canadian Field-Naturalist* 61:116.

Currah, R. S. and M. van Dyk. 1986. A survey of some perennial vascular plant species native to Alberta for occurrence of mycorrhizal fungi. *The Canadian Field-Naturalist* 100 (3): 330-342.

Driver, E. A. 1987. Fire on grasslands—friend or foe? *Blue Jay* 45 (4): 217-225.

Drysdale, P. D. (ed.) 1983. Gage Canadian Dictionary. Gage Publishing Ltd, Toronto.

Edwards, J. and J. R. Jordan. 1992. Reversible anther opening in *Lilium philadelphicum* (Liliaceae): a possible means of enhancing male fitness. *American Journal of Botany* 79 (2): 144-148.

Ende, J. E. van den and M. G. Pennock-Vos, 1997. Primary sources of inoculum of *Botrytis elliptica* in lily. Acta Horticulturae. Volume 2. Issue 430: 591-595.

Ericksen, J. C. 1979. My adventures with lilies. *The Lily Yearbook of the North American Lily Society* 32: 71-73. Quotation cited is on page 71.

Fitter, A. H. and J. W. Merryweather. 1992. Why are some plants more mycorrhizal than others? An ecological inquiry. In: Read, D. J., D. H. Lewis, A. H. Fitter and I. J. Alexander (eds.) Mycorrhizas in Ecosystems. C-A-B International, Wallingford, UK, p. 26-36 .

Flock, E. B. 1942. Wild Flowers of the Prairie Provinces. School Aids and Text Book Publishing Co., Regina. Quotations cited are on page 61.

Fox, E. 1993. Growing to understand *Lilium philadelphicum*. *The Lily Yearbook of the North American Lily Society* 46:30-34. Quotations cited are on pages 31 and 34.

Francis, C. S. 1950. [Note] *Blue Jay* 8 (3):26.

Gayton, Don. 1990. The Wheatgrass Mechanism. Fifth House Publishers, Saskatoon. Quotation cited is on page 106.

Gilmore, M. R. 1919. Uses of Plants by the Indians of the Missouri River Region. 33rd Annual Report, Bureau of American Ethnology, Smithsonian Institution, Washington, D.C.

Grant, K. A. and V. Grant. 1968. Hummingbirds and Their Flowers. Columbia University Press, New York.

Hammermeister, A. M, D. Gauthier and K. McGovern. 2001. Saskatchewan's Native Prairie: Taking stock of a vanishing ecosystem and dwindling resource. Native Plant Society of Saskatchewan, Saskatoon.

Heath, F. W. 1963. Lady Slippers. *Blue Jay* 21 (4):163.

Hellson, J. C. and M. Gadd. 1974. Ethnobotany of the Blackfoot Indians. Canadian Ethnology Service Paper No. 19. National Museums of Canada, Ottawa.

Hind, H. Y. 1971 [1860]. Narrative of the Canadian Red River Exploring Expedition of 1857 and of the Assiniboine and Saskatchewan Exploring Expedition of 1858. Volume I. Originally published by Charles E. Tuttle Company, Vermont. Reprinted by M. G. Hurtig, Edmonton.

Hoffmeister, D. 1989. Mammals of Illinois. University of Illinois Press, Champaign, IL.

Houston, C. S. 2002. Spread and disappearance of the Greater Prairie-Chicken, *Tympanuchus cupido*, on the Canadian prairies and adjacent areas. *The Canadian Field-Naturalist* 116 (1):1-21.

Howie, V. 1964. Let's Grow Lilies: An Illustrated Handbook of Lily Culture. North American Lily Society.

Imper, D.K., G.E. Hovey, J.O. Sawyer, S.A. Carlson. 1987. Table Bluff Ecological Reserve Operations and Maintenance Schedule. Draft Reports to California Department of Fish and Game.

Jackson, H. H. T. 1961. Mammals of Wisconsin. University of Wisconsin Press, Madison, WI.

Kindscher, K. 1987. Edible Wild Plants of the Prairie. University of Kansas Press, Lawrence, Kansas.

Lajeunesse, C. 1996. Surveying. In: Canadian Encyclopaedia Plus (CD rom version), McClelland and Stewart, Toronto.

Lalond, A. N. and M. A. Pedersen. 1999. Administration of Dominion Lands 1870-1930. In: Fung, K. (ed.) Atlas of Saskatchewan. University of Saskatchewan, Saskatoon, pp. 48-49.

Lamb, W. K. 1957. Sixteen Years in the Indian Country: The Journal of Daniel Williams Harmon, 1800-1816. MacMillan Company, Toronto.

Leighton, A. 2000. Buzzing ball baffles botanist. *Blue Jay* 58(2):104.

Lockwood, J. A. 2004. Locust. Basic Books, New York. Quotation cited is on pages 26-27.

Macoun, J. 1883. Manitoba and the Great North-West. Thomas C. Jack, London.

Macoun, J. 1895. 'J. Macoun to Hon. T. M. Daly, November 21, 1889.' Canada Department of the Interior, File Number 123293. In: Raby, S. 1966. Prairie Fires in the North-west. *Saskatchewan History* XIX (3): 81-99, pp. 94-99.

Macoun, J. 1979 (1922). Autobiography of John Macoun, M.A.. Second Edition. Ottawa Field Naturalists' Club, Ottawa.

Moerman, D. E., 2002. Native American Ethnobotany. Timber Press, Portland, Oregon.

Morrison, D. 1948. The Prairie Lily. School Aids and Text Book Publishing Company Ltd, Regina.

Nader, G. A. and W. K. Setter. 1969. Transportation in Saskatchewan. In: Richards, J. H. and K. I. Fung (eds.). Atlas of Saskatchewan. University of Saskatchewan, Saskatoon, p. 174.

Olson, J. 1991. Native Lily Conservation in Wisconsin. *The Lily Yearbook of the North American Lily Society* 44: 74-78.

Parfitt, E. E. 1957. *Lilium philadelphicum* in Wisconsin. *The Lily Yearbook of the North American Lily Society* 10: 76-77.

Pennell, F. W. 1936. Travels and scientific collections of Thomas Nuttall. *Bartonia* 18:1-51.

Pfeiffer, N. E. 1960. A bouquet of thoughts on lilies. *The Lily Yearbook of the North American Lily Society* 13: 7-10. Quotation cited is on page 8.

Plant Physiology On Line Topic 23.5:Types of Seed Dormancy and the Roles of Environmental Factors. http://www.plantpphys.net/article.

Priestly, I. M. 1945. Report on the Western Red Lily. *Blue Jay* 4 (1):2.

Priestly, I. M. 1946. Information Please. *Blue Jay* 4(2): 23.

Raby, S. 1966. Prairie fires in the northwest. *Saskatchewan History* 19:81-99.

Raup, H. M. 1934. Phytogeographical studies in the Peace and Upper Liard River regions, Canada, with a catalogue of the vascular plants. Contributions of the Arnold Arboretum of Harvard University, No. VI.

Richards, B. 1968. Record Lily. *Blue Jay* 26 (1):61.

Richardson, J. 1823. Botanical Appendix. In: Franklin, John. Narrative of a Journey to the Polar Sea in the Years 1819-20-21-22. John Murray, London, pp.729-763.

Rockwell, F. F., E. C. Grayson and J. de Graaf. 1961. The Complete Book of Lilies. Doubleday & Company, Garden City, New York.

Roe, F. G. 1970. The North American Buffalo. Second Edition. University of Toronto Press, Toronto.

Rowe, J. S. 1990. Home Place: Essays on Ecology. NeWest Publishers, Edmonton. Quotation cited is on page 161.

Salt, J. R. 1976. Seasonal food and prey relationships of badgers in east-central Alberta. *Blue Jay* 34(2):119-122.

Savage, C. 2004. Prairie, A Natural History. Greystone Books, Vancouver.

Sawatzky, H. L. 1979. Prairie potholes. *Blue Jay* 37 (1):3-8.

Schuster, J., 2001. Botrytis (gray mold): a disease for many plants. http://www.urbanext.uiuc.edu/hortihints (Accessed August 18, 2004).

Scott-Brown, J. M. 1977. Stoney Ethnobotany: An Indication of Cultural Change Amongst Stoney Women at Morley, Alberta. Master's Thesis, University of Calgary.

Seton, E. T. 1909. Life-histories of Northern Animals. Volume 1: Grass Eaters. C. Scribner's Sons, New York. Quotation cited is on page 526.

Shaw, C. C. 1947. General Notes. *Blue Jay* 6 (1): 8.

Shaw, C. C. 1948. [Note] *Blue Jay* 6 (2):31.

Silcox, D and V. L. Harms. 1989. The yellow immaculate lily in Saskatchewan and adjacent Manitoba, and its persistence in native lily patches. *Blue Jay* 47 (2): 69-73.

Skinner, M. W. 2002. Lilium. In: Flora of North America Editorial Committee (ed.) Magnoliophyta: Liliidae: Liliales and Orchidales. Volume 26, Flora of North America North of Mexico, Oxford University Press, New York, pp. 172-197.

Southesk, The Earl of (James Carnegie). 1875. Saskatchewan and The Rocky Mountains. Edmonston and Douglas, Edinburgh.

Spry, I. M. (ed.) 1968. The Papers of the Palliser Expedition 1857-1860. The Champlain Society, Toronto.

Sullivan, J. 1991. A Lily of the Canadian Prairies. *The Lily Yearbook of the North American Lily Society* 44: 82-83.

Synge, P. M. 1980. Lilies: A Revision of Elwes' Monograph of the Genus *Lilium* and its Supplements. Universe Books, New York. Quotations cited are on pages 185 and 235.

Thacker, C. 1953. A Remarkable Lily. *Blue Jay* 11 (3):18.

Thornton, F., J. Bowman and D. Struthers. 1993. Agricultural policy review part 2: Wheat Board Quota System. *Blue Jay* 51(2):65-71.

Torrey, B. and F. H. Allen (eds.) 1962. (Dover Edition). The Journal of Henry D. Thoreau. Volumes 1 & 2. Dover Publications, New York.

Trottier, G. C. 1991. Conservation of Canadian Prairie Grassland: A Landowner's Guide. Environment Canada, Ottawa. Quotation cited is on page 53.

Vogl, R. J. 1974. Effects of Fire on Grasslands. In: Kozlowski, T. T. (ed.) Fire and Ecosystems. Academic Press, New York, pp. 139-194.

White, T. (ed.) 1886. Descriptions of the Townships of the North-West Territories. MacLean Roger & Co., Ottawa.

Woodcock, H. B. D. and W. T. Stearn. 1950. Lilies of the World: Their Cultivation and Classification. Charles Scribner's Sons, New York. Quotations cited are on pages 26 and 25.

World Wildlife Website. The nature audit, Part II: Grassland habitat accounts. http://wwf.ca/About WWF/ What We Do/ The Nature Audit/The Nature Audit. (Accessed January 2004.)

References consulted for North American distribution information shown on page 14

Barkley, T. M. et al (eds.)1991. Flora of the Great Plains. University of Kansas Press, Lawrence, Kansas.

Bergman, H. F. 1913. Flora of North Dakota. Tribune, Bismarck, North Dakota.

Correll, D. S. and M. C. Johnston. 1970. Manual of the Vascular Plants of Texas. Texas Research Foundation, Renner, Texas.

Deam, C. C. 1940. Flora of Indiana. Department of Conservation, Indianapolis, Indiana.

Dorn, R. D. 1977. Manual of the Vascular Plants of Wyoming. Garland Publishing, New York.

Dorn, R. D. 1984. Vascular Plants of Montana. Mountain West Publishing, Cheyenne, WY.

Fassett, N. C. 1959. Spring Flora of Wisconsin. Third Edition. University of Wisconsin Press, Madison, Wisconsin.

Fernald, M. L. 1970. Gray's Manual of Botany. D. Van Nostrand Company, New York.

Harrington, H. D. 1964. Manual of the Plants of Colorado, Second Edition. The Swallow Press, Chicago.

Marie-Victorin, E. C. Frère. 1964. Flore Laurentienne. Deuxième Edition. Les Presses de l'Université de Montréal, Montréal, Québec.

Mohlenbrock, R. H. and D. M. Ladd. 1978. Distribution of Illinois Vascular Plants. Southern Illinois University Press, Carbondale and Edwardsville, Illinois.

Ownbey, G. B. and T. Morley. 1991. Vascular Plants of Minnesota: A Checklist and Atlas. University of Minnesota, Minneapolis, Minnesota.

Packer, J. G. 1983. Flora of Alberta. Second Edition. University of Toronto Press, Toronto.

Porsild, A. E. and W. J. Cody. 1980. Vascular Plants of Continental Northwest Territories, Canada. National Museums of Canada, Ottawa.

Rydberg, P. A. 1922. Flora of the Rocky Mountains and Adjacent Plains. P. A. Rydberg, New York.

Rydberg, P. A. 1932. Flora of the Prairies and Plains of Central North America. New York Botanical Garden, New York.

Scoggan, H. J. 1978. The Flora of Canada. Part 2. National Museums of Canada, Ottawa.

Smith, E. B. 1988. An Atlas and Annotated List of the Vascular Plants of Arkansas, Second Edition. E. B. Smith, Fayetteville, Arkansas.

Straley, G. B., R. L. Taylor and G. W. Douglas. 1985. The Rare Vascular Plants of Eastern British Columbia (Peace River District, Columbia River Valley south from Kinbasket Lake), Syllogeus No. 59. National Museums of Canada, Ottawa.

Stevens, W. C. 1948. Kansas Wild Flowers. University of Kansas Press, Lawrence, Kansas.

Voss, E. G. 1972. Michigan Flora. Cranbrook Institute of Science, Bloomfield Hills, Michigan.

Wooton, E. O. and P. C. Standley. 1972 (1915). Flora of New Mexico. Volume 7. In: Cramer, J. (ed.) Reprints of US-Floras.

Provincial flag

The lily is prominently displayed upon the provincial flag that was officially dedicated on September 22, 1969. The flag is divided into two horizontal portions: a green half representing Saskatchewan forests; a yellow half symbolizing prairie wheat fields. The upper corner nearest the staff features the Coat of Arms (Armorial Bearing) adopted in 1906. The red colour of the lion facing the observer on the horizontal gold band across the upper third of the Shield signifies the fires that swept the prairies before and during settlement. The three golden sheaves of wheat cut the lower two-thirds into equal spaces of vertical green that represent the luxuriant grasses and other vegetation. Finally, the fly portion of the flag (the half farthest from the staff) bears the provincial floral emblem, with its flame-coloured petals.

The basic design was the creation of Anthony Drake of Hodgeville. It was one of over 4,000 entries in a province-wide flag design competition.

Coat of Arms

The Coat of Arms depicted here with supporters and crest was granted in 1986. The design incorporates many Red Lilies. How many can you find? The scroll with the motto MULTIS E GENTIBUS VIRES (from many peoples comes strength) is entwined with lily flowers. The standards supporting the shield are the lion representing the British heritage and the white-tailed deer (the provincial mammal). If you look closely the deer sports a pendant with a Red Lily. (This seems quite appropriate since deer are very fond of lilies!) A red maple leaf adorns the shoulder of the lion. Just beneath the crown is the animal symbol of Canada, the beaver, which to our knowledge doesn't eat lilies but is holding a lily in its paw.

Provincial legislation pertaining to the Red Lily.

Saskatchewan has three legislative acts that concern the Red Lily as the provincial floral emblem.

1. *The Floral Emblem Act, 1941*, assented to on April 8, 1941.

2. *The Floral Emblem Act, 1981*, assented to on December 12, 1980.

3. *The Provincial Emblems and Honours Act*, Chapter P-30.2 of the Statutes of Saskatchewan, 1988-89, effective as of June 29, 1988.

Copies of the three *Acts* are available from the Office of the Queen's Printer in Regina. The principal parts that pertain to the Red Lily are presented here.

    The Floral Emblem Act, 1941 states that "The flower known botanically as *lilium philadelphicum andinum*, and popularly called the 'prairie lily,' is adopted as and shall be the floral emblem of the province."

    The Floral Emblem Act, 1981, which superseded the previous *Act*, states that "The flower known botanically as *Lilium philadelphicum* L. var. *andinum* (Nutt.) Ker *andinum* and called the 'western red lily' is the floral emblem of Saskatchewan." This *Act* also details prohibited activities, exceptions to these and the fine for violation as follows:

"3. No person shall pick, cut down, dig, pull up, injure or destroy, in whole or in part, whether in blossom or not, the plant that produces the flower that is the floral emblem of Saskatchewan.

"4. Section 3 does not apply to any person:

(a) engaged in the lawful carrying out of any public work or of his occupation; or

(b) engaged in the carrying out of necessary work on property owned or lawfully occupied by him.

"5. - (1) Every person who contravenes this Act is guilty of an offence and liable on summary conviction to a fine of not more than $50.

(2) No proceedings under this section are to be instituted except with the consent or under the direction of the Attorney General."

The *Provincial Emblems and Honours Act* contains much the same information as the *The Floral Emblem Act, 1981*, but raises the maximum allowable fine from $50 to $500:

"(3) Any person who contravenes subsection (1) is guilty of an offence and liable on summary conviction to a fine of not more than $500." (Page 6, *The Provincial Emblems and Honours Act*).

Red Lily species, varieties and forms

Red Lily   *Lilium philadelphicum* L.

This species has many common names in western Canada: prairie lily, tiger lily, red lily and wood lily.

The two varieties of the Red Lily are

1 - the western variety: *Lilium philadelphicum* L. variety *andinum* (Nutt.) Ker.

2 - the eastern variety of the Red Lily: *Lilium philadelphicum* L. variety *philadelphicum*

The spotless yellow form of the western variety of the Red Lily is
    Lilium philadelphicum L. variety *andinum* (Nutt.) Ker. forma *immaculatum* Raup

The yellow form of the eastern variety of the Red Lily is
    Lilium philadelphicum L. variety *philadelphicum* forma *flaviflorum* Williams

Other plant species mentioned by common name in this book

Ascending purple milk-vetch   *Astragalus striatus*
Aspen poplar   *Populus tremuloides*
Chokecherry   *Prunus pensylvanica*
Harebell   *Campanula rotundifolia*
Highbush cranberry   *Viburnum opulus*
Little bluestem   *Andropogon (Schizachyrium) scoparium*
Michigan lily   *Lilium michiganense*
Northern bedstraw   *Galium boreale*
Paper birch   *Betula papyrifera*
Pine lily   *Lilium catesbaei*
Prickly-pear cactus   *Opuntia polyacantha*
Saline shooting star   *Dodecatheon pulchellum*
Skeletonweed   *Lygodesmia juncea*
Smooth brome grass   *Bromus inermis*
Smooth camas   *Zygadenus elegans*
Spreading dogbane   *Apocynum androsaemifolium*
Thorny buffaloberry   *Shepherdia canadensis*
Vetch   *Vicia americana*
Wolf willow   *Elaeagnus commutata*

Kirigami is the art of paper cutting that involves some initial folding of paper to allow a repeated design. You are probably familiar with making paper snowflakes or paper doll chains. Flowers are particularly suitable subjects for kirigami art, for there are many natural variations in petal shape. You may wish to give your lily crenulated or notched petals (see photos on facing page) and, like snowflakes, the uniqueness of the cutting adds to the charm. This craft is suitable for young and old alike.

Choose a square of coloured paper. Origami paper that is 14 cm (6 inches) square is a good size to work with.

Folding steps:

1. Fold in half, keeping the colour on the inside.

2. Using A as the centre point, fold along AB and align the left side of the base with AC.

3. Fold along line AC so that the right side of the bottom edge lines up with line AB.

4-6. The folded paper is now ready for your own petal design. Draw the petal shape onto the side of the folded paper and cut out. When you open the cut folded paper you will have a unique lily flower. A sample petal design (with a stamen to cut out in the centre) is provided in Step 5 below.

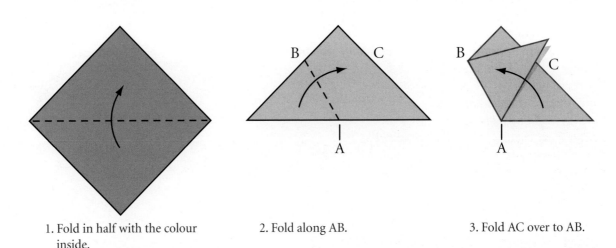

1. Fold in half with the colour inside.

2. Fold along AB.

3. Fold AC over to AB.

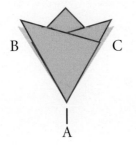

4. The folded paper is ready for your own design.

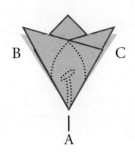

5. Cut along dotted line.

6. Unfold and discover your paper lily.

This page shows four variations in petal shape, colour and number that we have seen as we looked for and at lily flowers. The following page features developmental anomalies.

(1) Notched petals are not uncommon and the notching pattern varies from plant to plant. Here two petals, deeply-notched near the bottom, look like mittens. Often the notch is higher up along the edge of the petal and often the notches occur on both sides of the same petal.

(2) Wavy or crenulated edges are also seen but less often than notches.

(3) Only once have we come across a flower that had petals and sepals with clearly different shades of colour like this one with light apricot petals and dark apricot sepals.

(4) The fourth flower breaks all the rules of lilies. It has flower parts in series of four rather than three: four petals, four sepals, eight anthers and a four-lobed stigma. This was the only flower like this in the area where it was growing in the Strawberry Hills east of Saskatoon.

These remarkable Red Lily flowers show what can happen when things go wrong.

The 'pinwheel' seen from the side.

The sepals remained attached at the tip of this flower bud when it opened, creating a lily 'pinwheel.' Photographed near Bittern Creek on Highway 2, July 8, 2004.

Three petals are all that remain on this flower that has lost its sepals to disease, possibly botrytis blight. Photographed at Besnard Lake, July 8, 2004.

A four-petaled flower? Actually there are six petals/sepals, but two are riding piggyback on two others, making what looks like a perfect four-petaled flower. Photographed along Kilmeny Road east of Saskatoon, July 19, 2004.

General comments

Lilies are plants of temperate origins requiring a 'winter' or resting stage. Their development will follow an annual cycle of growth followed by a rest in a cool place. Some lilies, such as the Asiatic varieties commonly grown in prairie gardens, can be forced into earlier growth and blooming if the bulb is given a cold treatment of eight or more weeks, thus shortening the resting season.

Red Lilies (*Lilium philadelphicum*) grow from seed or bulb scales. The good news is that our native lily is easy to propagate; the bad is that you have to be patient in waiting for a flower to appear. Note: seed collected from specimens growing in the Alberta foothills may flower in two years (See the article by Jim Sullivan recommended below); generally, plants grown from seed in Saskatchewan take four or more years to produce a flowering plant.

Propagation from seed

For commercial seed sources, check with the Native Plant Society of Saskatchewan (www.npss.sk.ca). Alternatively, collect seed from private land (with the landowner's permission) in late September or October to ensure that the seed is fully ripened. In order to find the seed pods, stake blooming lilies in late June or early July. Make sure you stake several plants as some may not set seed and some may have been eaten. We can guarantee you will be challenged to find the pods if they aren't flagged.

Unlike in cultivated plants, seed germination of wild Red Lilies is unlikely to be higher than 90% due to genetic and environmental variables. Some seeds will germinate under just about any conditions: dark, light, (covered and not covered); immediate and delayed (one author recorded germination after 405 days!); cold treated or not. About 30% will germinate if you just sprinkle them onto a growing medium, such as a soil-less mix that has been pre-soaked (See Jim Sullivan's article). To maximize germination we suggest that you first wash the seed. This can be done by putting the seeds in a tea ball or similar porous enclosure and suspending it in your toilet tank. The seeds will be automatically washed every time the toilet is flushed. A week of washing is more than adequate. (This technique also works well for hard-to-grow seeds like parsley.)

Place the washed seed on the pre-soaked growing mix in a deep pot or seedling (forestry) tray. Cover very lightly with a little dry growing mix. Firm the soil, cover with plastic and then place in a refrigerator for 6 to 8 weeks (in other words use a standard cold stratification technique). Alternatively, put dry seed into the refrigerator for 6 to 8 weeks and plant as just described.

The first growth, a slender, grass-like cotyledon will emerge in about two weeks. When the seed germinates, the rootlet grows downward and the node nearest the seed elongates, growing upwards and turning green. The seed coat is often dragged with it when it emerges as a loop before it straightens. This first leaf looks like a blade of grass and there is only one—lilies, like grasses, orchids, bamboos and others classed as "Monocotyledons" produce only one (mono) seed leaf (cotyledon).

Once the plants are growing it is best to keep them in a greenhouse or under grow lights for several months. If planted out they may not get adequate moisture to ensure growth. You will notice a series of small true leaves, about 1 to 1.5 cm long, indicating the development of a small bulb. After a growing period of about four months, the plants can be transplanted into the garden or you may wish to continue growing them by using a series of cool rest periods at 5 to 7° C for three months, followed by three- to four-month periods of growth. This regime was used by Shand Greenhouse to accelerate bulb growth. Once the plant produces its first stalk, it should be transplanted to a permanent location in early fall or mid-May. Remember that in the wild the plant takes at least four years to mature or for the bulb to grow to the size that will produce the first flowering stalk.

Transplanting

Site preparation

Lilies need some direct sunlight. Use 'Where to look,' in Chapter 10 as a guide to where to plant. In nature, Red Lilies grow under a wide variety of soil conditions from acidic to alkaline and from gravelly, sandy to sand-silt loam with some clay. Heavy clay soils need to be amended with coarse material and lots of humus (peat moss, leaf mold or compost or a combination of these). Humus is an excellent addition to all soils to encourage root growth. A humus-rich, friable soil worked to the depth of 22 cm (9") would be good for growing lilies. Lilies need good drainage. A 10-15 cm (4-6") layer of soil mixed with some coarse sand needs to be placed in the rooting zone that starts about 5 cm (2") below the soil surface. If the site is prone to standing water or water-logged soils, plant the bulbs in a slightly raised bed or on a slope.

Plant companions

Red Lilies do not compete effectively with many plants. Make sure that the planting area is weed free. Do not plant in the same area as plants that have a sprawling mat-forming style of growth (e.g., yarrow, pussytoes). However, lilies do need some protection, as bare soil is prone to baking and cracking. A top dressing of peat moss or fibrous compost will be beneficial. If the planting is a native flower garden, we suggest the following plant associates which grow with the Red Lily as it occurs in natural habitats: Harebell (*Campanula rotundifolia*), Saline Shooting Star (*Dodecatheon pulchellum*), Northern Bedstraw (*Galium boreale*), American Sweet Vetch (*Hedysarum alpinum*), Meadow Blazingstar (*Liatris ligulistylis*), Star-flowered Solomon's Seal (*Smilacina stellata*), Early Blue Violet (*Viola adunca*), Smooth Camus (*Zygadenus elegans*) and Meadow Parsnip (*Zizia aptera*). For recent sources of seed and plants, check the Native Plant Society website (www.npss.sk.ca).

Planting depth and spacing

The general rule is that the larger the bulb, the deeper it is planted. A bulb 2 cm (3/4") in diameter should be planted in a hole such that the bulb is positioned about 5 cm (2") deep. Top dress lightly. Space bulbs about 30-50 cm (12-18") apart. Water well after planting to encourage rooting. Both spring and fall are good times to plant.

Rescuing lilies about to be destroyed

The following advice from A. R. Brown appeared in the 1955 *Lily Yearbook*: "Many lily enthusiasts claim to have had difficulty in transplanting and naturalizing the Prairie [Red] Lily, but that was not my experience. Using a good steel trowel I cut the turf deeply around the bulb and lifted out the blooming plant with a cone of soil, then rolled it in newspaper for carrying home. If the cut is wide and deep enough, the bulb and roots are not seriously disturbed. At home I set the cones back into a natural position in the soil but made sure there was gravelly loam drainage underneath and a layer of peat or turf on the surface. They survived and flowered quite naturally as long as those two conditions of good drainage and surface peat protection were maintained."

To this good advice we would add: if the roots are damaged in digging, the plant will stop growing for that season. Early fall is probably the safest season for transplanting but you will have to flag the plant in July. Water well to encourage root development.

Long-term Survival

The jury is out regarding the necessity for the presence of mycorrhizal fungi in garden-grown lilies. Under natural conditions these fungi have been found in the roots of the Red Lily, however, all the soils were also nutrient compromised. In garden conditions with adequate moisture and nutrient rich soils, the presence of these fungi is not likely critical, but the final word awaits more research into this area. Some growers such as Mr. Brown (above) have cultivated the Red Lily successfully; others have seen a decline and disappearance.

Disturbance (fire, small mammal tunnelling) is an important factor in maintaining vitality. We suggest that every three to five years, once the bulbs are large enough to produce flowers, you move the bulbs or disturb the ground around the plants. Remove and burn the old lily stems in the fall to minimize the presence of botrytis blight.

As to advice on fertilizing lilies: in our research plots we have seen lilies growing right through the edge of a cow pie with no evidence of ill effects. Based on this observation, a top treatment of manure may be just the stimulus they need to really thrive.

Recommended Reading

A good general and entertaining booklet on lily growing is *Let's Grow Lilies: An Illustrated Handbook of Lily Culture* by Virginia Howie. It is available through the Canadian Prairie Lily Society. Their web site address is www.prairielily.ca

Saskatchewan lily grower, Jim Sullivan, writes of some of his experiences on growing *Lilium philadelphicum* var. *andinum* in an article entitled *A Lily of the Canadian Prairies*, published in 1991 in *The Lily Yearbook of the North American Lily Society* 44: 82-83.

No... A-1 ... Page... 22

Date... 4 JN 03

No.....................

Date.....................

9:00 cool overcast, slight breeze
9:45
Job 1: checking planting — see planting notebook
The planting area well used by mice — there was
last winters
a mouse nest on tag 5-1, plus 2 other nests
in the planting m² plus lots of tunnels, and
collections of shredded veg. too small to be voles.
An ideal habitat created by hoof + root
exclosures.

Job 2: complete plot survey. T at 9:45 = 11°C
higher at 11:50 - 12°C

A) 98-02   V 10
   98-01   N, 6 st (5)
   95-03   N
   95-02   N
   95-01   B, 9
B) 01-086 N
   01-087 V 14
   95-04   N
   96-01   N
D) 95-06   N
   95-05   N
   97-21   N

Very dense now with thatch
abundant small mammal activity.
Small plug on small mammal droppings filling a shallow depression

SORA, COOT, YHBL, RWBL, WEME
Shooting stars tall, abundant, scattered.

E) 97-22   N
F) 96-02   N
   96-03   B,
   97-23   N
G) 98-03   N
(101) 02-01 B
   96-04   N
H) 97-24
   96-05
J) 95-07
K) 95-08
L) 98-04

Field notebook page, June 4, 2003.

138